THE little
HASTINGS
FISH
COOK BOOK
3

FIRST EDITION
PUBLISHED 2014

ISBN 978-0-9563663-2-3

© **Sea Saw Books**
West Villa 1 Victoria Road St Leonards on Sea
East Sussex TN37 6ER

THE little HASTINGS FISH COOK BOOK 3

SALLY WALTON

Illustrations by Stewart Walton
Design by Debi Angel

SAW
books

Author's note

This is the third Little Hastings Fish Cook Book to be published
by Seasaw Books.

We want to support the fishing community by encouraging people
to buy the local catch from a fishmonger or the fishing huts on the beach.
We asked Hastings and St Leonards residents (and some regular visitors)
to contribute their tried and tested, favourite recipes using only
locally caught and sustainable fish. We only bent our rules slightly to
include smoked haddock – caught elsewhere, but smoked locally.

This fresh little book features delicious new recipes,
an up-to-date reference section of places to buy and eat fish
plus a selection of the best recipes from Books 1 and 2.

...ver sole with ...own butter and ...tercress

...ply, simply, simply is ... way you need to cook ...ver sole. Best caught ... the south coast from ...over to Hastings, it's a ...licate fish that we ...ould enjoy more often. ...is delicious cooked ...hole and on the bone ...nd eaten with brown ...utter to add a touch of ...itterness to the dish.

SERVES TWO

INGREDIENTS

2 tbsp plain flour
1 Dover sole, filleted
3 tbsp olive oil
200g butter
Juice of 1 lemon
Small bunch of flat-leaf parsley, chopped

To serve
Small bunch of watercress

METHOD
□ Line a sieve with muslin and rest it over a bowl. Spoon the flour into a shallow dish and season well. Dip the fish fillets

into the flour and coat well, then shake briefly to dust off any excess.

☐ Heat a large, non-stick frying pan over a medium heat until hot. Add the oil, swirl it around to heat it, then lay the sole fillets into the pan.

☐ Cook the fish for one to two minutes until golden (you may need to lower the heat slightly at this stage, so the pan doesn't become too hot) then flip the fillets over and cook on the other side for one to two minutes more. Pop on to a warmed plate.

☐ Put the pan back over a medium heat and add the butter. Cook until the butter turns nut brown – it's ready when it smells nutty – then take the pan immediately off the heat and strain through the muslin-lined sieve.

☐ Stir the lemon juice and parsley into the butter in the bowl, then spoon over the fish and serve straightaway with the watercress alongside.

Recipe from *James Martin's Great British Adventure* by James Martin (Quadrille, £25)

DEDICATION

IN MEMORY OF GRAHAM COGLAN

who spent over 40 years as

skipper of his boat

Alfie Elliot RX60.

We dedicate this little book to Graham

and all Hastings fishermen,

whose low-impact fishing

methods help to protect

the marine environment.

Coastal communities like theirs

are as endangered

as some of the fishes in the sea

and they deserve everyone's support.

In Hastings we are very lucky to have
four individual fishmongers plus a
row of fish huts at the top of the beach,
all selling freshly caught local fish.
A traditional Londoner's daytrip
to Hastings wouldn't be complete
without a visit to the fishmonger to place
an order that'd be name-tagged and put in
the fridge to be picked up on the way home.

Hastings fishmongers always welcome the
visitors but it's worth remembering
that it's only the locals that will keep them
in business from day to day.
So please ignore the so-called convenience
of buying fish in a supermarket and go for
the experience of getting to know
your local fishmonger instead.

Be more experimental when buying fish –
it's all too easy to buy what's familiar
but far more interesting to ask questions
and try new flavours.
It's so much more fun shopping
inquisitively everyday like we do
on our holidays. Ask what's just in,
choose sustainable and local,
and savour the freshness and flavour.

YOU WON'T REGRET IT –

& NEITHER WIL

HE FISHMONGERS
OR THE FISHERMEN.

Small is beautiful...

...but our small boats need a bigger share of the fishing quota.

Hastings fisherman Paul Joy would rather be on his boat but these days he spends much of his time speaking on behalf of those who put to sea in small boats measuring less than 10m in length. The problem lies in the allocation of fishing quotas – literally the amount of each fish species that a fleet is allowed to catch. Quotas were introduced to protect dwindling fish stocks and prevent overfishing but in reality they give an unfair advantage to the big fleets. While bigger boats have quotas so large they rarely reach them, small boats from coastal communities are struggling to make a living because their quotas are unrealistically small.

Hugh Fearnley-Whittingstall's Fish Fight campaign was successful in highlighting the issue of discards – the netted fish that has to be literally thrown over the side before the boats come ashore, so as to not exceed quotas. Following the campaign, the EU has now banned discards with effect from 2015/16.

Our artisanal fishing fleets
are so much more than a tourist attraction,
so please give the fishermen your support
and help to keep our historic
coastal communities alive.

However, introducing the ban without increasing small boat quotas is actually going to leave small boat fishermen even worse off than they are now.

Unless the quota system is changed to allow them more flexibility, the changes won't help our local fishermen to survive. With the discard ban coming in they will have no option but to land the whole catch. Any fish that isn't the right size to sell, or which is outside the quota, will have to be processed into fishmeal and this will cost them money. Despite the rustic nature of their daily lives they face the same market pressures as any other business.

Sustainability is the message they would like us to pass on. That means choosing fish that are naturally plentiful, whose stocks are not threatened by overfishing. We need to eat a variety of fish too – if we all start eating pollock instead of cod, the two fish will simply swap places on the endangered list. And as it happens, we have an abundance of cod in this area and almost no pollock at all.

TIPS FROM PAUL AT ARCADE FISHERIES

Please support your local fishmongers, we have the freshest fish and are always happy to advise on what is seasonally best and to fillet fish while you wait. Supermarkets are good for a lot of things but they're no place to buy fresh locally caught fish.

BUYING FISH:
What to look for when buying fish:
1. CLEAR BRIGHT EYES
2. CLEAN, CHERRY RED GILLS
3. FIRM FLESH THAT SPRINGS BACK TO THE TOUCH.

DE-SCALING FISH:
Lay the fish flat, hold the head and use the back of a blunt knife to stroke firmly from tail to head.
Do this underwater to avoid scales flying everywhere – if using a sink make sure the plughole has a mesh filter!

MACKEREL: Wash the fish in salted water and be sure to clear away any dark blood from inside the fish as it will give the fish a bitter taste.

MAKE STOCK: Always ask the fishmonger for bones to make your stock – they're always happy to help.

FISH STOCK OR COURT BOUILLON

When the fishmonger fillets your fish ask him to give you a bag of bones, head and tail. When you get home, rinse under a cold tap and put in a pot. Cover with water and boil then skim off any scum that forms on the surface. Add a peeled sliced onion, a clove or two of garlic, parsley with stalks and a bay leaf. If you want to spice it up, add a sprinkle of chilli flakes. Simmer for 25 minutes and strain.

To freeze, boil hard to reduce the stock by half then freeze in ice cube trays.
Once frozen these can be bagged up and labelled so that a couple of cubes can be used at a time to add flavour to any fish stew or sauce.

THE LOCAL CATCH

DOVER SOLE ⚓ PLAICE ↴
DABS ♦ COD ↯ HUSS ∿ SKATE ⟋
MONKFISH ⌢ SQUID ✲
MACKEREL ⚓ HERRING ♪
SPRATS ⚊ SEABASS ✕
GREY MULLET ⟋
GURNARD ⟋ SEA BREAM ⟋

Not forgetting the shellfish....

LOBSTER ✺ CRAB ♦ BROWN
HRIMP ✿ & RAZOR CLAMS ⚱

(if you're very, very lucky)

And a few that are ALMOST local ......

OYSTERS FROM WHITSTABLE
CLAMS FROM POOLE
SCALLOPS FROM RYE

And a super-seasonal treat...

AMPHIRE – THIS SUCCULENT GREEN PLANT
GROWS ON THE COASTAL MARSHES,
SO ITS NOT SURPRISING THAT IT GOES
SO WELL WITH FISH.

IMPORTED WHEN OUT OF SEASON HERE,
SO ALWAYS ASK TO TASTE A SPRIG BEFORE YOU BUY.
IT SHOULD NOT BE TOO STRINGY, WOODY OR SALTY.

FRYING FISH: A QUICK GUIDE

It's easy to master the art of perfect fried fish.
Our simple guide covers the secrets of getting a really
crisp skin, adding texture and flavour with different
coatings and batters, and choosing the right oil for
the occasion.

FIRST, THE BASICS...

Plain and simple fried fish is most delicious when you
make a feature of the sizzled skin. Dry the fish thoroughly
and make sure pan is well oiled and hot before gently
putting the fish in skin side down for 80% of the
cooking time then turn it over to brown the other side.
If you come over all cheffy you can press the fish down
as the skin fries to get the most even and crispiest result.

ADD A LITTLE EXTRA SOMETHING...

Coating fish creates a barrier between the hot fat and the
skin or flesh, helping to keep the fish moist as it cooks.
Here are a few ideas – you can add extra flavours to any
of them. Try fresh herbs, grated Parmesan, cayenne
pepper or smoked paprika.

SEASONED FLOUR: The simplest coating of all.
Use on its own, or as a first step before, say, coating with
one of the batters below. For an extra-crisp coating, dust
the fish with flour then beaten egg then flour again.

FRESH BREADCRUMBS: Place cubed bread in
a food processor or blender and whizz to a fine even
crumb. Make sure the oil is hot when you add the fish or
the soft crumbs will absorb it, become heavy and drop
off the fish.

DRIED BREADCRUMBS: Break stale bread into
chunks and dry slowly in an oven set to a low
temperature: the aim is to remove the moisture, not cook
the bread. Put the dried out chunks in a blender and
whizz til fine and even.

KNOW YOUR OILS...!!!

Whichever oil you choose, make sure it's fresh. Oil can be reused several times for chips, but never for fish as it absorbs and retains flavours.

Groundnut: A great neutral oil to use when you want the flavour of the fish to shine through.

Sunflower: An all-purpose cooking oil with a golden colour. Great for fish and chips – although aficionados swear by lard or dripping.

Rapeseed: Great for low-cholesterol diets. The organic oil has a strong colour and nutty flavour.

Olive oil: Light olive oil is best for frying and perfect for Mediterranean dishes. Save the extra-virgin stuff for salads or drizzling over the finished dish.

COATING FISH FOR FRYING

PANKO CRUMBS: These Japanese crumbs are made from crust-less white bread and give a very crispy coating. They can be bought at Oriental grocers and most big supermarkets.

POLENTA (CORNMEAL): Polenta makes a crunchy corn-flavoured coating. Nice with salsa!

OATMEAL: This is a traditional coating for herrings in Scotland and is just as good for other oily fish like mackerel or sardines. Dip the fish in milk then oatmeal. The oatmeal will absorb the oil and develop a nutty flavour when fried to a crisp.

BEER BATTER: This makes a good basic fish-frying batter.
200g self-raising white flour
330ml cold lager
Pinch of sea salt. Sift the flour into a bowl and pour in the lager, whisking until you have a smooth batter with the consistency of double cream. Dry the fish then coat it in batter and deep fry.

TEMPURA: This is a very light Japanese-style batter. If you don't want to make your own, a packet of tempura mix gives pretty good results.
250ml iced fizzy water
150g self-raising white flour
Whisk the batter ingredients lightly and use it straight away. The oil must be hot to make the batter dipped pieces puff up.

> **Tip**
>
> **BUTTER** is delicious for frying sole, or very fresh plaice fillets. It burns easily on its own, though, so always add a small amount of oil too.

& TO GO WITH YOUR FISH...

Fish flavours are usually subtle, so it's best to choose accompaniments that won't overpower the star of the show. Looks count too, so put some colour on your plate. A sprig of parsley with a slice of lemon, a bright red tomato salsa or some vibrant mushy peas will please the eyes and the tastebuds.

SIDE DISHES
MUSHY PEAS:

A softie Southern version of the up-North standard. An essential accompaniment to fish and chips.
450g packet of frozen peas, cooked and drained
Salt and pepper
Small cup chicken stock
A big squeeze of lemon
A handful of fresh mint
> Blend together for 30 seconds or less so the peas turn to a mush but not a purée.

GRATED COURGETTE:

Grate a courgette or two, sprinkle with salt and leave to drain in a colander for 30 minutes. Rinse under a cold tap then dry using kitchen paper or a clean tea towel, making sure you squeeze out all the moisture. Melt a knob of butter in a pan and gently fry a clove of crushed garlic, then add the courgette and stir it into the garlicky butter. Cook for a few minutes then serve spoonfuls with grilled fish.

LEMON MASH:

Peel and boil floury potatoes then mash with butter and season as usual. Add the finely grated rind of one unwaxed lemon. Lovely with pan-fried, roasted or grilled fish.

THAI-STYLE CUCUMBER SALAD:

Peel a cucumber and slice it length-ways into sticks, removing the seeds. Put into a bowl and cover with 2 chopped shallots or a small chopped red onion and a red chilli cut in fine rounds. Mix up a dressing as follows: put 1 cup of rice or white wine vinegar, ½ a cup of water, ½ a cup of sugar, a pinch of ground turmeric and a crushed garlic close in a small pan and heat until the sugar dissolved. Pour over the cucumber and serve. Any leftovers will keep in a glass jar for two weeks.

OVEN-BAKED POTATO WEDGES:

So easy to make, and a million times better than the frozen type. Cut medium-size potatoes in half and par-boil for 8 minutes. When cool enough to handle cut them into fat wedges. Put 2 tbsp of good olive oil in a bowl with salt and good grating of black pepper (or try smoked paprika for a change or some sprigs of rosemary). Tip the potatoes in and mix them round until completely coated.
Heat the oven to 200°C (Gas Mark 6). Arrange the potato wedges thin side up on a shallow oven tray and bake for 30 minutes or until golden.

TOMATO, CELERY AND SPRING ONION SALAD:

The secret is to chop everything super fine.

Serves 2

2 large ripe tomatoes (de-seeded and skinned if you like)

2 sticks of celery – use a potato peeler to de-string it

6 spring onions

Salt and pepper

Juice of a lemon

Olive oil

(same volume as lemon juice)

Basil is an optional but very nice extra

> Sharpen your knife and chop all the ingredients into a very fine dice. Mix up a dressing of oil and lemon, pour over and season. Nice straight away or refrigerate for the next day. Lovely with boiled new potatoes and any grilled or pan-fried fish.

SAMPHIRE:

We are so lucky in Hastings because samphire grows locally and is often on sale at our favourite fishmongers. Succulent and salty, it's the perfect accompaniment to local fish. It's versatile too: try it raw, steamed, in salads, or stir-fried in butter with garlic. There are no rules, so enjoy experimenting with this gift from the marshes.

BEETROOT RELISH:

Great with any grilled fish. Add a bunch of watercress for a real colour pop.

2 beetroot

1 small onion, chopped

1 tsp peeled and chopped fresh ginger

1 tbsp hot horseradish

> Boil beetroot until soft. Put the beetroot, onion and ginger in a blender with the horseradish and blend until smooth.

Lorna Lloyd, The Printworks B&B, Hastings

Samphire

Tip

Pour a kettle of boiling water over the samphire then drain and eat with butter and black pepper.
Gail, Rock-a-Nore Fisheries

SAUCES, SALSAS, DIPS & DRESSINGS

BASIC VINAIGRETTE

Try using different oils to change the flavour, or add a bit of extra zing with a splash of pomegranate syrup or Hastings Ketchup.
30ml white wine vinegar or lemon juice
10ml grainy or Dijon mustard
175ml oil – try olive, walnut, cobnut, rapeseed or sunflower
Salt and pepper
> Whisk the mustard and vinegar together very thoroughly and season with salt and pepper. Pour in the oil and whisk to a creamy texture.
OR Put all the ingredients into a jar, screw the lid tightly and shake vigorously.

SAUCE PORTUGAISE

A garlicky, tomato sauce with a chilli kick, that's good with oily fish.
50ml olive oil
1 medium onion finely sliced
2 x cloves of garlic crushed
½ tsp dried chilli flakes or a de-seeded fresh chilli
1 x tin tomatoes
bay leaf
half a glass red wine
salt and black pepper
> Pour oil into a saucepan, add onion and cook gently till transparent. Add garlic and chilli and cook for another minute. Add the tomatoes, bay leaf and the wine. Simmer till it has reduced and thickened.

BUTTER BEAN & GARLIC PUREE

Try this as an alternative to mashed potato with crisply fried flat fish.
1 x tin of butter beans
30ml olive oil
4 cloves of garlic crushed
1 tsp finely chopped rosemary
Pinch of red chilli flakes
1 tbsp lemon juice
salt and pepper
> Warm the olive oil, chilli, half the garlic and the rosemary in a pan Puree the beans in a blender then add the oil mixture. Blend. Add the rest of the garlic, the lemon juice salt and pepper.

Tip

HASTINGS KETCHUP:
A little fanfare please for a true local food hero: Hastings Ketchup. The little bottle with the lemony Worcestershire sauce is made right here and is available from local fishmongers and delis. It's hard to imagine life – or fish! – without it.

DIPPING SAUCE

This is equally good for delicate steamed fish or fritters

2tsp rice wine vinegar /Mirin
2 tsp sugar
1-2 small red chillies
1-2 tbsp light soy sauce
1 tsp toasted sesame seeds
> Heat the vinegar and sugar in a small pan. Add the chilli once the sugar has dissolved. Leave to cool in a bowl then add sesame seeds and soy sauce just before serving.

SAMBAL

2 ripe tomatoes
½ red onion
1 green chilli
(remove seeds if you don't like heat)
1 small cucumber
¼ cup coriander
¼ cup mint
½ tsp salt
4 tbsp white wine vinegar
4 tbsp lemon juice
> Finely chop the tomatoes, onions, cucumber, chilli, mint and coriander by hand or quickly in a food processor – don't overdo it though, you want a fine dice not a pulp. Mix everything together with lemon juice and vinegar, and leave to marinate in a sealed bowl in the fridge for an hour. Taste and add more vinegar if necessary. Add more salt if it's too sour.

ROUILLE:

The classic accompaniment for fish soup.

4 garlic cloves, crushed
1 medium red chilli, deseeded and roughly chopped
1 large red pepper
½ tsp smoked paprika
180ml olive oil
2 tbsp fresh white breadcrumbs
> Roast the red pepper in the oven at 200°C until it softens and the skin is slightly charred.
Remove the pepper from the oven and peel off the skin with a small knife.
Halve the pepper, remove the seeds and roughly chop the flesh. Place the garlic, chilli, red pepper and smoked paprika in a food processor or blender and purée to a smooth paste. With the motor running, gradually pour in the olive oil until well combined. Finally, blend in the breadcrumbs. Season the rouille to taste. You can make this in advance and keep it in the fridge for up to a week.

Paul Webbe, Webbe's Rock-a-Nore and The Fish Café Rye

PIER NINE'S HERB-ROASTED BREAM WITH MOROCCAN SPICED CHICKPEAS AND MINT YOGHURT

Fresh whole bream (or sea bass)
400g tin chickpeas, drained and rinsed
Fresh coriander, mint and dill
1 lemon
1 clove garlic, crushed
A few slices of orange and fennel (or use shallot if fennel isn't available)
Extra virgin olive oil
100g fresh tomatoes and 100g chopped tinned tomatoes
A little tomato purée
½ glass dry white wine
Saffron
Dried cumin, ginger, coriander and smoked paprika

Pier Nine's herb-roasted bream with Moroccan spiced chickpeas and mint yoghurt

You can scale this recipe up or down, according to the size of your fish. As a general guide, a 400-450g whole fish will feed one person generously. The quantities given here for the chickpeas will feed up to 4 as a side dish.

Preheat oven to 180°C (Gas Mark 4).

Gut and scale the fish (if the fishmonger hasn't already done it for you). Wash the cavity and season well with salt and pepper. Stuff with slices of orange, fennel and soft herbs such as tarragon, dill or parsley. Score the fish on each side 3 times, cutting down to the bone and with even spacing. Season generously with salt and pepper, and place on oiled baking parchment. Drizzle with extra virgin olive oil and place in the oven for around 8 minutes. Turn the fish over and return to the oven for a further 6-8 minutes.

For the chickpeas, mix together the spices and fry gently in oil. Add the crushed garlic and fry for a minute. Add wine, and cook for another minute before adding the chopped and fresh tomatoes, tomato purée and saffron. Cook for a further 2 minutes. Add chickpeas, cook for a minute or two and add chopped coriander and lime juice. Taste and adjust seasoning as required.

For the yoghurt, finely chop mint and stir into the yogurt along with a pinch of cumin and a pinch of sugar, then season with salt and pepper.

20

Pier Nine Restaurant, Zanzibar Hotel, St Leonards on Sea

FISH BAKED IN PAPER
(PSARIA STO KHARTI)

1 whole large fish –
black bream, plaice,
lemon sole or sea bass
2 lemons
Salt
Oregano
Garlic
Olive oil

Artist Peter Waldron and his wife Lois divide their time between Hastings Old Town and a small village in Crete, which gives their recipe a Grecian flavour.

Prepare the fish – gut, remove the scales and clean – or ask to have this done. Place the fish on 2 sheets of greaseproof paper that you have lightly oiled. Add a little crushed garlic and oregano to the inside of the fish plus a squeeze of lemon juice. Squeeze the rest of the lemon juice over the outside of the fish plus a drizzle of olive oil.

Fold the fish up in the paper and secure the ends tightly with string. Place the parcel on a baking tray and put in a moderate oven for about an hour – this should be about right for a fish weighing 1kg or a bit more. Serve off the bone and skinned.

Lovely served with a dressing. Mix equal quantities of oil and lemon juice (125ml) plus 2 tablespoons of chopped parsley, salt and pepper.

Peter and Lois Waldron

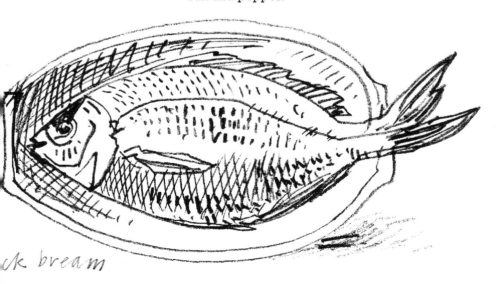

TONY'S FABULOUS FISH SOUP

For the stock:
First go down to Rock-a-Nore, ask for Gail, flutter your eyelashes and ask for a couple of fish carcasses – any white fish will do, including heads.
Smoked haddock skin is good too
200g crab claws (or buy a crab, eat the meat and keep the legs and shell)
½ pint prawns, shells on
1 fennel bulb, roughly chopped
2 sticks celery, roughly chopped
1 red chilli, chopped
2 cloves garlic, chopped
1 onion, roughly chopped
2 tbsp olive oil
2 tbsp plain flour
A glug of Pernod
A glug of white wine
A squeeze of tomato purée
Salt and black pepper
Water to cover

I normally do this soup when I have an open house for Jack in the Green – it's easy to scale up to feed a crowd. It's a bit of a faff to make, but it's amazing – trust me.

Serves 8
Using a large pan, sweat off in olive oil the fennel, onions, garlic, fennel, celery and chilli till just soft. Add fish carcasses (roughly chopped up), crab shells/claws (smashed up) and the prawns.
Add flour and gently mix to coat all ingredients.
Add Pernod and white wine, then enough water to cover.
Season well. Bring this to a simmer and gently cook for around an hour.
Fish stock doesn't take long, so set the timer.

While the stock is cooking, peel and chop the potatoes into quarters. Put these in a pan of salted water and cook till just done. Have your fish pieces ready in a separate bowl and your whole prawns on a baking tray ready for the oven.

When the stock is ready, sieve it through a colander into a separate pan pushing down the bulky matter to get all the flavour out.

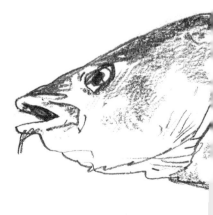

For the rest:
500g fish pie mix (ask
for it without salmon)
½ a side smoked haddock,
skinned, pin boned and
cut into 2cm cubes
500g waxy potatoes,
such as Charlotte
8 jumbo prawns, whole
with shells on (adds a bit
of wow to the finished dish)
8 tbsp brandy

Tony Howard,
Hastings Old Town

Now sieve again, pouring the stock back into the original pan. Discard any bits. Put the sieved stock back on the heat and bring to a gentle simmer. Mix in tomato purée till it has a nice pink colour.

Pop the whole prawns into the oven and roast till pink. These will go on the individual bowls when serving.

Add the potatoes to the stock, return to a simmer, then add your fish. When it comes back to a simmer again, turn the heat off and leave for a few minutes so as not to overcook the fish.

23

Serve in big pasta bowls with a tablespoon of brandy floated on top and one of the roasted prawns for garnish.

TA DAH! ENJOY ...
IT'S THE BUSINESS.

TO ADD A BIT :
OF WOW TO THE FINISHED DISH
8 TBSP BRANDY

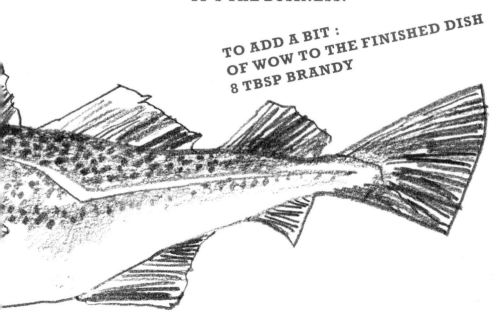

MONKFISH CURRY

1 medium onion
1 block coconut milk or ½ a tin
1 medium fillet of monkfish
1 red pepper
Fresh ginger fresh
Fresh garlic
Curry powder, medium to
hot depending on your taste
Fresh coriander
Rapeseed or vegetable oil
Water

Heat 1 tbsp of oil in a large pan and fry the chopped onion. Cut the monkfish into cubes and add to the onion. Add 1 or 2 chopped cloves garlic, and the sliced red pepper. Add 2 level tbsp curry powder. Cook for 15 minutes, then add the coconut milk and grated fresh ginger, and cook for another 5 minutes. If it seems too thick add a little water. Sprinkle with fresh coriander and serve with jasmine rice.

Lize McCarron,
St Leonards on Sea

REMEMBER: CURRIES ARE ALWAYS BETTER THE NEXT DAY!

DRUNK SPRATS

The title doesn't refer to the sprats, which are absolutely stone cold sober. Rather, it's a reference to the craving that one might get after indulging in a few glasses of vino. At times like this there's nothing more delicious than a bowl of these crunchy fish with fresh bread and perhaps a bit more vino to wash them down.
Do take care when frying fish as the oil is very, very hot!

A bowl of sprats
Another bowl with a cup of
flour for coating
Light olive oil and a wok
Mayo, lemon, chilli sauce or
whatever you fancy

Helen Robinson, SHOP,
Norman Road,
St Leonards on Sea

Tip the sprats into the flour and shake them about till they're well coated. Heat the oil till just about smoking and gently tip in the sprats. Move them about till they're a lovely golden colour then remove and drain them on kitchen paper. Eat while they're sizzling hot.

CRAIG'S WHITEBAIT

More of a mouth-watering story than a recipe...

I was on the beach this afternoon when there was a 'mackerel boil' – an event where a shoal of mackerel surrounds a shoal of baby herrings (whitebait) and the sea explodes with the little critters jumping from the mackerel's jaws. It was close to shore and loads of whitebait were washed on to the shingle.
I found a plastic cup and packed them in. Although normally vegetarian, this counts as 'roadkill' and I suspended my principles in favour of my appetite for rare treats. Dusted in oat flour (a nod to the fact that if they had survived they would have eventually swum to Scotland) and salt, sizzled in olive oil now their Omega 3s are me.

Craig Sams,
Hastings Old Town

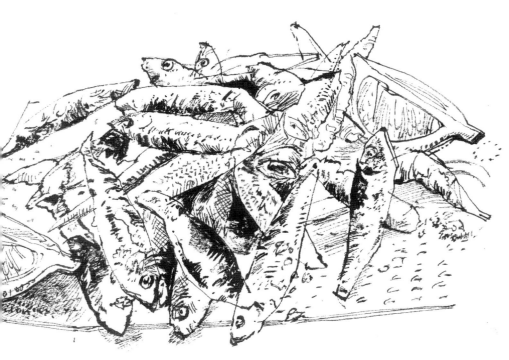

Craigs whitebait

MALAY HAWKER'S MONKFISH

1 whole monkfish tail
4 shallots
1 large garlic clove
2 large pieces
fresh turmeric
Thumb-size bit of ginger
About 20 curry leaves
1 or 2 birds' eye chillies
1 tbsp coriander seeds
1 tbsp cumin seeds
1 tbsp palm sugar
1 tbsp fish sauce
Tin of coconut milk

Josh George,
Hastings

Toast the whole spices until they start to pop, then grind to a fine powder. Put the shallots, garlic, turmeric, chillies and ginger in a food processor with a splash of the coconut milk and blitz.

Cut the monkfish into 2.5cm pieces, season and fry in a hot wok until they have a bit of colour, then remove. Turn the heat down and put in the spices, paste and curry leaves. Stir fry until the paste starts to colour and the curry leaves give off their amazing aroma, then add the monkfish, coconut milk, palm sugar and fish sauce and allow to simmer. Check seasoning.

Serve with steamed jasmine rice sprinkled with some extra fried curry leaves.

26

GRANDMA'S FISH PIE

**600g undyed
smoked haddock
5 eggs
900g potatoes
1 small onion, chopped fine
4 cups milk
1 tbsp plain flour
25g butter
Salt and pepper
Curry powder to taste
Chopped parsley**

*Lionel Copley,
Swan House
& The Old Rectory,
Hastings Old Town*

Serves 4
Preheat oven to 180°C (Gas Mark 4).

Boil and then mash potatoes with butter and milk. Poach fish in milk until nearly cooked Remove fish, leave to cool, then skin and bone, saving liquor. Hard boil eggs, then shell and chop into chunks. Make the sauce with flour and butter and the fish liquor, add milk if necessary to form a smooth creamy consistency. Fry onion in a little butter until clear.
Add curry powder to taste. Pour over the fish, place in large pie dish,
cover with potato, flake butter on top.
Bake for 35 minutes, or until golden brown.
Serve sprinkled with a generous amount of chopped parsley

27

THE BEACH HUT COOK'S CLAM AND CHORIZO STEW

1 tbsp oil
1 large onion,
peeled and finely chopped
1 large carrot,
finely chopped
1 stick celery,
finely chopped
3 garlic cloves, crushed
300g chorizo,
chopped small
1 jar pasta sauce
(try Lloyd Grossman's
Roasted Garlic & Tomato)
Salt and pepper
1 tsp dried oregano
Good pinch sugar
1kg clams
1 large glass dry white wine
Fresh parsley, chopped

The Beach Hut Cook,
food blogger

Serves 4

Heat a large saucepan and add oil. Fry the onion, carrot and celery for a good 5 minutes, then add the garlic and continue to cook for a further 5 minutes until softened but not browned. Add the chorizo and give the mixture a good stir. Cook for a couple of minutes to allow the chorizo oil to introduce itself to the onion mixture, then add the pasta sauce, salt, pepper, oregano and sugar. Cook for 20 minutes.

In a separate saucepan bring the wine to a boil, add the clams and cook for 4 minutes. Discard any that haven't opened. Take off the heat and remove about three -quarters of the shells. Pour the clams, along with the cooking liquid, into the tomato sauce and cook for a couple of minutes until all warmed through. Scatter over the fresh parsley.

Serve with chunky, crispy bread so you can get every last bit of it.

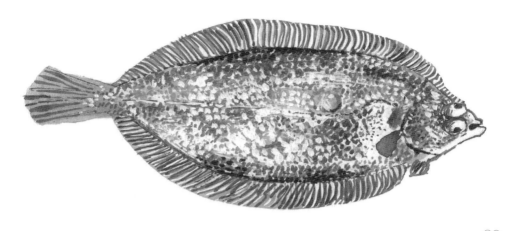

BAKED FISH WITH A CHEESY CRUMBLE

450g pollock
or other white fish
1 egg
50g freshly grated
Parmesan cheese
150g dried breadcrumbs
Seasoned flour
50g butter plus extra
for frying

Dave Watkins
St Leonards on Sea

Preheat oven to 200°C (Gas Mark 6).

Coat fish with flour. Melt butter in frying pan, brown fish on both sides. Mix 50g butter, breadcrumbs and cheese to make a crumble. Beat the egg in a bowl and dip the fish in it. Cover fish with crumble mix and bake in a hot oven for 8 minutes or until lightly browned.

GRILLED SPICED MACKEREL WITH FENNEL COLESLAW

4 local fresh mackerel
fillets, pin boned
75g Greek yoghurt
75g mayonnaise
2-3 tsp creamed horseradish
1 large fennel bulb, halved,
thinly sliced, fronds too
1 green apple,
cored and thinly sliced
1 large carrot, grated
1 stick celery, including
leaves, thinly sliced
¼ tsp ground cumin
¼ tsp ground coriander
1 tbsp roughly torn
coriander leaves
for garnish
Salt and cracked
black pepper to taste

Lisa Sapire, Hastings Old Town

Preheat the grill to medium/high.

To make the coleslaw, mix the yoghurt, mayo and horseradish in a bowl. Add the fennel, apple, carrot and celery and mix. Leave for at least 10 minutes to let the flavours develop.

Mix the spices together, then sprinkle over the fillets, rubbing it in to the flesh. Place the fillets skin-side up on a lightly oiled baking tray and grill for 4 minutes. Then turn over and grill the other side for 2-3 minutes more so the fish is cooked through.

Serve the grilled mackerel fillets on the homemade coleslaw and garnish with the roughly chopped coriander.

SEA BASS WITH POTATOES, ANCHOVIES AND LEMON

*only ok. Not a good
idea to add stock to
Sou+le ,
potatee*

4 sea bass fillets
600-700g waxy potatoes
(Charlotte or Anya)
cleaned and cut into
1cm discs lengthways
12 anchovy fillets
1 tbsp capers, drained
1 large lemon cut in wedges
4 tbsp olive oil
150ml vegetable stock
Sea salt and black pepper

*Jane Scruton,
Hastings Old Town*

Preheat oven to 200°C (Gas Mark 6).

Warm the olive oil in a roasting tin over a hot-ish flame. Put the potatoes in until pale gold on both sides. Add the lemon wedges, anchovies and capers and pour over the stock. Transfer to oven and cook until the potatoes are almost done (30 minutes)

Lay the fish fillets over the top of the potatoes skin side up and drizzle with a little olive oil, season with salt and black pepper. Bake for about 10 minutes until the fish is cooked and the skin is crisp and brown.

Serve with green beans or a tomato salad.

BUTTERFLIED HERRINGS

4 butterflied herrings

Dressing:
4 tbsp olive oil
2 tbsp wholegrain mustard
Large bunch basil
1 tsp clear honey
Zest and juice of a lemon

Stephanie Donaldson,
Hastings Old Town

First make the dressing: roughly tear basil leaves and combine them with the other dressing ingredients.

Set grill on its highest setting, brush the herrings with oil, place them skin side up on the grill tray and season lightly before grilling for 6 minutes or until the skin blisters. Place herrings on serving plate and immediately spoon the dressing over the hot fish.

100g cockles
300g steamed chopped spinach
225g sour cream or crème fraîche
225g mayonnaise
Freshly ground pepper
2 garlic cloves, crushed
1 tsp Tabasco (or to taste)
1 tbsp Worcestershire sauce
Smoked paprika
1 large loaf of sourdough bread

Kristina Alexander, Hastings

SPINACH AND COCKLE DIP

Steam the chopped spinach and set aside to cool. Squeeze all the liquid from the spinach (or you will have watery dip). Place in a medium size bowl and combine with the remaining ingredients (except the bread).

Garnish with smoked paprika and serve with cubes of sourdough bread on the side for dipping.

Lime

ANGEL'S TOP OF THE RAINBOW SQUID

Enough squid for 2
120g fresh egg noodles
2 tsp good olive oil
1 big garlic clove,
peeled and crushed
1 or 2 red chillies
1 yellow & 1 orange pepper,
deseeded and thinly sliced
2 courgettes, thinly sliced
2 handfuls baby spinach
or samphire, if in season
Zest and juice of ½ a lemon
or lime

A colourful, quick and easy way with squid. A delight of colour, the red, orange, yellow and green are the colours of the top part of the rainbow. Ask one of our hunky Hastings fishmongers to clean and prepare the squid for you.

Heat oil in a wok or deep pan, add the peppers, garlic and then the courgettes. Meanwhile cook the noodles in boiling water. If you're using samphire, drop it into the pan for the final minute of cooking time. Drain and refresh under cold water.

Add the squid to the wok/pan, and toss/ move around for a couple of minutes, then follow with chillies, adding the spinach at the end until it's just wilted. Add the lemon/lime zest and juice and season as required. Serve ASAP. When finished go and get more or invite a friend.

Debi Angel,
St Leonards on Sea

32

squid

GEFILTE FISH BALLS

50g haddock fillet, skinned
50g cod fillet, skinned
1 medium onion
2 eggs
2 tsp salt
Pinch of pepper
2 tsp sugar
1 tbsp oil
50g matzo meal
(most supermarkets
stock it)

This is a traditional Jewish recipe.

Wash and salt the fish and leave to drain for half an hour.

Peel and chop the onion into chunks. Put into the food processor with eggs, seasoning and oil and mix to a smooth paste. Pour into a large bowl, stir in the matzo meal and leave to swell.

Cut fish into 2.5cm chunks and put into the food processor half at a time. Process for 5 seconds to chop the fish very finely. Add to the matzo mix and blend together by hand. The mixture should be firm enough to shape into a ball the size of a small apple. If it's too firm add a bit of water; if it's not firm enough add some more matzo meal.

To fry the fish balls, pour about 2.5cm of oil into a frying pan and heat. Carefully lower the fish balls into the oil and fry gently, turning often so they are evenly browned. Equally delicious served hot or cold.

Samara Streeten,
Hastings Old Town

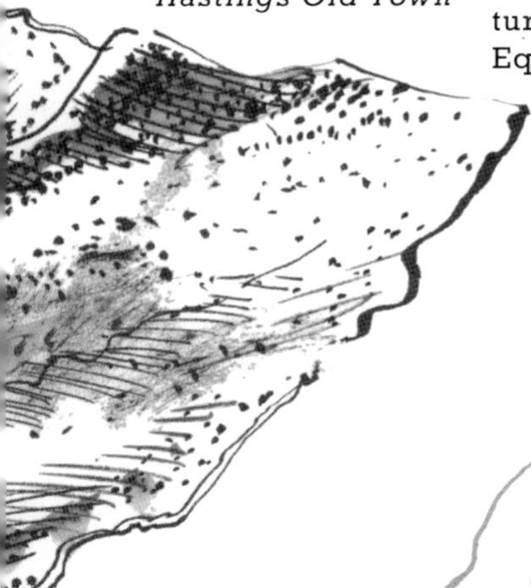

33

SARAH'S SEA BEET
AND SMOKED MACKEREL
FILO TARTLETS

Makes 8 little tarts

75g cooked Hastings smoked
mackerel
A good handful sea beet,
chard or spinach
3 sheets filo pastry
2 beaten eggs
150ml single cream
2 tbsp vegetable oil or
melted butter
Black pepper

These delicious little tarts are made with wild sea beet (Beta vulgaris maritima), the parent of chard and beetroot. Commonly found growing around the coast, hardy sea beet grows in rosettes of glossy, green, pointed leaves which are quite variable in shape. They look like spinach, but thicker and fleshier. The leaves are rich in vitamins A and C and antioxidants and minerals, and have a rich, earthy flavour with a hint of the sea, although they taste a bit soapy when raw! For extra flavour you could add a few crushed fennel seeds or lemon zest, maybe parsley or wild chervil, chives or wild garlic, but I like the tarts au naturel.

Be judicious with your foraging: only take what you need, spread your picking around several plants, and leave enough leaves behind for the plant to regenerate – especially as other people might be picking in the same area. Avoid the larger, tattier leaves. Always use a good plant identification book as some very common plants in the UK are highly poisonous – if you're in any doubt, leave it out!

Preheat oven to 180°C (Gas Mark 4).

Wash your sea beet leaves well and spin in a salad spinner or dab dry with kitchen paper. Remove stems and trim out any particularly thick leaf midribs then chop fairly roughly.
Flake the mackerel and remove any bones. Mix the beaten egg and cream well and add a good grinding of black pepper.
Cut your filo into strips about 8 x 13cm and brush one side of each with the olive oil or melted butter. Lay one strip into a hole of a muffin tin, lay another strip at an angle, then overlap the third strip so the base and sides of the hole are covered.
You may need to scrunch the tart edges up a bit to separate them.
Divide your sea beet and smoked mackerel flakes between the tart cases and pour over most of the egg and cream mixture.
Poke the tart filling with a fork to get rid of air spaces and top up with the remaining egg and cream mix.
Pop in the oven for 15-20 minutes or until the pastry is crisp and golden and the filling just set. Leave to cool for a few minutes then transfer to a wire rack. Enjoy while still warm – perhaps with a foraged salad

A final word of warning: avoid low growing plants where people walk dogs...If you can't find any sea beet, use spinach or chard instead.

Sarah Watson, Hastings.
www.wildfeast.co.uk

PARMESAN DOVER SOLE WITH LINGUINE

2 fillets Dover sole, plaice or dabs, depending on the money in your purse on the day!
1 cup flour mixed with 1 cup finely grated Parmesan cheese
1 cup seasoned plain flour
1 beaten egg for coating fish
1 heaped tbsp capers
Lemon juice
Knob of butter
Generous splash of white wine

This very simple fish recipe is not posh and doesn't take long to make but has great flavour, so it's a good supper dish for all those time poor cooks! I was served Parmesan sole and linguine in Sardinia at a roadside café where service had finished but they took pity on hungry English travellers! This recipe is based on my memory of that dish.

Dust the fish in the seasoned flour, dunk in the beaten egg, then coat with the flour and parmesan mix and shallow fry on both sides in a pan with some olive oil until golden. Remove the fish to a warmed serving dish or plates,

Add the knob of butter and capers to the pan and swish around on the heat, squeeze in your lemon juice plus a good splash of wine and season with freshly milled black pepper. Spoon some of the sauce over the fish.
Serve with linguine glazed with the rest of the sauce.
A few extra shavings of Parmesan can't hurt!

Susan Elliot,
St Leonards on Sea

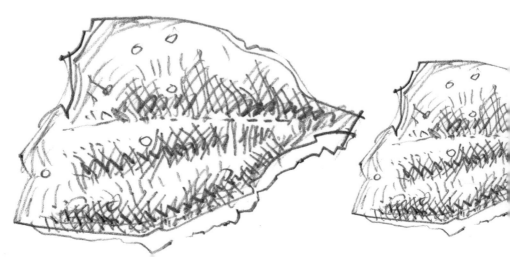

HUSS FISH FINGERS

1 chunky piece of skinned huss
1 egg
A few slices of bread (or bought crumbs if you're short of time.)
oil for frying

Most people love a convenient fish finger but if you want something to cook with kids this is both easy and fun and there's a good chance they'll enjoy eating them too. I made them with a group of under 10's at the Rye Bay Beach School and they were a great success. Huss works well for these as its plentiful, has no small bones, holds its shape when cut and is already quite square, so there's very little wastage.

Cube the bread and place in a baking tin in a low oven to dry out for 15 minutes. When it's cool put it in a freezer bag, squeeze the air out and tie up the end. Use a rolling pin to whack it into crumbs – this part is very popular with kids.

Break the egg and beat it in one of the bowls. Tip the crumbs into the other bowl. Use a sharp knife to cut the fish into fingers – the usual size. Dip the fingers into the egg then roll them in the crumbs. Put them on a wire rack to dry out. Shallow fry in oil then drain on kitchen paper

Sally Walton,
St Leonards on Sea

Serve in a sandwich with crispy lettuce or watercress, or alongside a salad with ketchup or mayo for dipping.

MRS SOLIMAN'S EGYPTIAN FISH TAGINE

500g firm white fish,
cut into chunks
A handful of cooked prawns
Olive oil
1 large, thinly sliced onion
½ a clove of garlic, chopped
1 tin of chopped tomatoes
1 tin of chickpeas
2.5cm piece of fresh
grated ginger,
1 hot chilli,
finely chopped.
Use the seeds too
if you like it fiery.
1 tsp each turmeric,
cumin and cinnamon
(or 3 tsp of ras-al-hanout,
the ready-mixed tagine
spices sold at any good
Middle Eastern grocery.
Omit the chilli
if you use this)
Sea salt and black pepper
to taste
1 tbsp honey
7cm strip of apricot leather,
or a handful of dried apricots
A handful of dried golden
sultanas or chopped dates

Mary Long,
St Leonards on Sea

Have fun with this one – Egyptians cook by eye, not measuring spoon. You can manage the thickness of the sauce by adding water, but remember to bung in more spices if you do so. If you like it thicker, add more fruit.

Serves 4

Fry the onion and garlic in the olive oil gently until soft (but not brown). Add the spices and stir for a couple of minutes, then add the tomatoes and the dried fruit and 500ml water. Keep the heat medium-low and cook gently, stirring occasionally, until the gravy thickens. Drain the chickpeas, add and let them absorb the flavour for a few minutes, then add the fish and prawns and honey. Cover the pan and simmer gently until the fish is cooked through but still tender. Season to taste and serve garnished with a dollop of seasoned yogurt and some toasted hazelnuts. Best with fresh flatbread or buttery couscous.

BRAZILIAN COD
WITH COCONUT

**600g skinned
cod fillets, cubed
2 tbsp olive oil
1 large Spanish onion,
finely sliced
4 spring onions, trimmed
and chopped
2 cloves of garlic,
crushed
1 green chilli, seeded
and finely chopped
1 green pepper, sliced
400g tinned
chopped tomatoes
3 tbsp finely chopped
fresh parsley
1 tbsp finely chopped
fresh coriander
Salt and ground
black pepper
350ml coconut milk
(either tinned, or
reconstituted creamed
coconut)
Boiled rice to serve**

*Nicki Davidson,
Hastings Old Town*

Heat the oil in a large flame-proof casserole. Gently fry the sliced Spanish onion. Add the spring onions, garlic, chilli and green pepper and cook for 2 minutes. Add the tomatoes and cook for 5 minutes. Stir in the parsley and coriander. Season to taste with salt and pepper.
Pour over enough of the coconut milk to make a thick sauce. Stir. Bring to a gentle boil, then reduce the heat and stir again. Add the fish fillets and simmer for 15 minutes. Check the seasoning again, and serve with rice.
Serves 6

40

SMITHS' BUTTERNUT SQUASH, SWEET POTATO & COD CURRY

2 cod loins, cut into 2.5cm slices or cubes
Olive oil
Thai red curry paste
Large handful cashew nuts or red-skinned peanuts
1 large butternut squash, peeled and cut into 2.5cm cubes
4 sweet potatoes, peeled and cut into 2.5cm slices or cubes
500-1000ml hot vegetable stock
1 400ml tin coconut milk
4 handfuls spinach, roughly chopped
1 lime

This autumn/winter dish is a firm favourite at *smiths* and can be adapted to suit all tastes. We use cod but it lends itself to most firm-fleshed white fish. The great thing about this dish is that it is all cooked in one pot, with no weighing of ingredients, so it's really easy to prepare.

Serves 4
Ideally use a heavy based pan or casserole dish that can go on the hob. Put a little olive oil in the pan and heat, then add Thai red curry paste and cashew or red-skinned peanuts and gently fry for 30 seconds. The amount of Thai red curry paste you use depends on the level of heat you like. Start with 4 tsp – you can always add more later. Now add the butternut squash and stir over a low heat, then add the sweet potato.

Once the butternut squash and sweet potato are coated in the curry paste and nuts, pour over the hot vegetable stock so the ingredients are just covered. Place a lid over the pan and leave to gently cook until the butternut squash and sweet potato are done. Now add the coconut milk, chopped spinach and cod loin.

Cook gently for another 10 minutes then add a good squeeze of lime juice. Take off the heat, cover with a lid and leave to sit for 5 minutes. Serve with rice and enjoy!

If you want to spice it up a bit, add a bit more Thai red curry paste: heat a little olive oil then add a teaspoon or two more of the curry paste (be careful as it will 'spit' as it cooks).
Cook for 20 seconds then add to the curry and gently stir in.

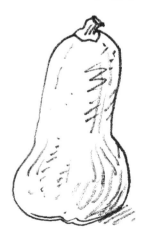

Richard Smith,
smiths realfood,
St Leonards On Sea

41

CORONATION MACKEREL

About 10-15 small waxy potatoes (such as Charlotte or Anya) either whole or cut in half if larger
3 hot-smoked mackerel fillets (might also work with hot smoked salmon fillets too but haven't tried this...)
250ml single cream (I use soya cream which works just as well and is less rich)
1 tbsp Dijon mustard
1 tbsp medium curry powder
Handful of fresh coriander and dill
Slug of olive oil

Nicole Collomb, St Leonards on Sea

42

I love the idea of coronation chicken – all those comforting cream and curry flavours and so simple. But being a 'fishatarian' I don't 'do' chicken, so here is a fish version my German friend Renate taught me that requires a strong tasting fish like smoked mackerel to really work.

Serves 4
Heat oven to 220°C (Gas Mark 7) and roast potatoes in olive oil, occasionally basting and turning them until golden (usually about 45 minutes). When the potatoes are cooked, skin and flake the hot smoked mackerel fillets evenly over the top of the potatoes. Pour the cream into a mixing bowl, add the Dijon mustard and curry powder and stir. Snip the fresh dill and coriander into the sauce and pour evenly over the fish and potatoes. Cover with foil and heat in the oven at about 200°C (Gas Mark 6) for about 20 minutes.
Delicious served with fresh steamed green vegetables or a crispy green salad.

MACKEREL OR SARDINE SALAD WITH WATERCRESS AND HARDBOILED EGG

For the fish:
8 x 60g mackerel fillets, slashed
100ml olive oil
Juice and zest of 1 lemon
Picked thyme leaves
2 cloves garlic, finely chopped

Salad:
3 bunches watercress picked, washed and properly dried

Vinaigrette:
80g chopped shallots
1 tbsp grain mustard
90g honey
20g sugar
1g salt
6 turns of fresh ground black pepper
90ml white wine vinegar
180ml vegetable oil
80ml olive oil

Tom Aikens, chef

Mackerel, sardine or herring will all work well in this recipe.

Serves 4
4 free-range or organic eggs, boiled for 9 minutes, cooled, shelled and cut in half or quarters

To make the vinaigrette, whisk the mustard, honey, vinegar, shallots, sugar, salt and pepper together, then slowly whisk in the two oils till the mixture is emulsified.

For the fish, mix all the ingredients together (apart from the fish!). Brush the mix on to the mackerel fillets and season.
Put the fish under the hot grill on a baking tray and cook for 4-6 minutes keeping slightly pink. Once the mackerel is cooked drizzle a little vinaigrette on top of the fish and leave to cool slightly

To finish, flake the mackerel and mix through the salad leaves with the egg quarters around the plate.

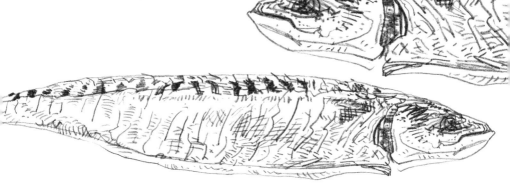

CATH'S JAPANESE CUTTLEFISH

Cuttlefish
Generous
big knobs of butter
vegetable oil
soy sauce

Cuttlefish are a local and sustainable fish catch around Hastings and they are in season from May. It's a great shame that cuttlefish is not widely available since it makes a great family meal – nutritious, low fat, and ready in a jiffy. It's a great substitute for squid, so we can eat like we're in the Med in Hastings! Like squid it needs either very fast cooking or stewing for over an hour. The more people ask for cuttlefish the more it will be stocked in the shops. This is a childishly simple recipe that's easy to adapt by adding your own favourite ingredients. You can also incorporate cuttlefish cooked this way into other dishes like paellas and pastas recipes. I can't vouch for its authenticity, but this is what I often did in Japan.

Get the fishmonger to prepare the cuttlefish (a very messy business). You should end up with a large 'hood' of rubbery white flesh and a few tentacles. Using a sharp knife, open up the hood. Score the flesh on the inside a few millimetres deep diagonally one way then the other, to create a cross-hatched pattern. This will speed up the cooking, help the cuttlefish absorb the flavours better and make it look pretty. Slice the cuttlefish into strips about 1cm wide and 5cm long.

Heat a little vegetable oil in a wide pan, add a good knob of butter and get it all hot. Throw in the cuttlefish and stir fry for about 30 seconds. The cuttlefish will quickly curl up. Add a few sloshes of soy sauce and a bit more butter and fry for another minute. It's ready!

Serve on rice or with noodles.

You can adapt and improve this recipe by adding your own favourite ingredients such as garlic, ginger, fish sauce, lemon, chilli etc. Garnish ideas include parsley, chopped spring onions or a handful of kastuoboshi (dried tuna flakes).

Catherine Tajima-Powell,
St Leonards on Sea

CULLEN SKINK

500g undyed smoked haddock, skin on
A bay leaf
Generous knob of butter (or two!)
1 large onion, peeled and finely chopped
leek, washed and cut into chunks
2/3 medium potatoes, unpeeled, cut into chunks
500ml milk (either whole or semi-skimmed)
250ml cream
Chives or parsley, chopped, to serve

Cullen skink is a thick soup made of smoked haddock, potatoes and onions, from the town of Cullen in Moray on the north-east coast of Scotland. It is often served as a starter at formal Scottish dinners. An authentic Cullen skink will use 'finnan haddie' – haddock smoked over green wood and peat in north-east Scotland – but it may be prepared with any other undyed smoked haddock.

Place the fish into a pan large enough to hold it comfortably, and cover with about 300ml cold water. Add the bay leaf, and bring gently to the boil. By the time it comes to the boil, the fish should be just cooked – if it's not, give it another minute or so. Remove the fish from the pan, and set aside to cool. Reserve the cooking liquid.

Melt the butter in another pan on a medium-low heat, and add the onion and the leek. Cover and allow to sweat, without colouring, for about 10 minutes until softened. Season with black pepper. Add the potato and stir to coat with butter. Pour in the haddock cooking liquid and bay leaf, and bring to a simmer. Cook until the potato is tender.

Meanwhile remove the skin and any bones from the haddock, and break into flakes. Lift out 2 generous slotted spoonfuls of potatoes and leeks and set aside. Discard the bay leaf. Add the milk, and half the haddock to the pan, and either mash roughly or blend until smoothish. Add the reserved spoonfuls of potatoes, leeks and the remaining fish.

Season to taste and when cool enough add the cream. Gently reheat to serve with a generous sprinkling of chives or parsley. Serve with fresh warm, crusty bread.

potatoes

Wendy Pritchett,
St Leonards on Sea

SCALLOPS WITH LIME, CORIANDER AND CHILLI

**6-8 scallops
out of the shell
1 tbsp olive oil
2 large crushed and
chopped garlic cloves
1 tsp chopped
fresh red chilli
Juice of ½ a lime
Small bunch roughly
chopped coriander
Salt and pepper**

*Sally Walton,
St Leonards on Sea*

A friend made this for us, and it was pure and simple bliss! It makes a perfect starter.

Serves 2

Fry the scallops in the olive oil for about 1 minute until golden, then flip them over and sprinkle the garlic and chopped fresh red chilli into the pan. Cook for about 1 minute more, then squeeze over the juice of the lime. Garnish with roughly chopped coriander and salt and pepper. Serve immediately.

46

shelled scallops

MOROCCAN FISH TAGINE

500g firm white
fish fillets such
as cod, huss or monkfish
3 carrots, sliced
1 onion, sliced
1 red pepper, sliced
4 plum tomatoes
8 new potatoes cut
lengthways
1 preserved lemon,
finely chopped
2 garlic cloves, chopped
Handful of olives
500ml fish or veg stock
1 cinnamon stick

Chermoula:
2 tbsp fresh coriander
3 garlic cloves chopped
1½ tsp cumin
1½ tsp paprika
1 tsp salt
½ tsp red chilli, seeded
½ tsp saffron
1 lemon, squeezed
4 tbsp extra virgin olive oil

*Nicole Collomb,
St Leonards on Sea*

This looks complicated as the list of ingredients is quite long but it's actually really simple. Just remember to leave time for marinating the fish first in chermoula, which makes it taste gorgeously exotic. Serves 4

Preheat oven to 180°C (Gas Mark 4) for First make the chermoula by blending all the ingredients in a mixer until smooth, then marinate the fish in the chermoula for at least an hour in the fridge. In the meantime, heat the oil in a large pan, add the carrot and onion and fry gently for 5 minutes until softened, not browned. Add the peppers, potatoes, preserved lemon, tomatoes, cinnamon stick and stock and bring to the boil then turn down heat and simmer for 30 minutes.

When ready, put the marinated fish in the bottom of a casserole dish (or tagine if you have one) and pour the cooked vegetable mix on top. Cover with foil or lid and cook for about 30 minutes or until the fish is cooked.

Delicious served with couscous mixed with chopped fresh parsley, coriander and mint and maybe a fresh mint tea.

47

CHINESE-STYLE SEA BASS

5 tbsp olive oil
5cm fresh ginger, peeled
and cut into thin strips
2.25 kg sea bass
1 small bunch of
coriander
18 small spring onions,
trimmed
2 tbsp sesame oil
2 tbsp tamari or
light soy sauce
Salt and pepper

Serves 6-8
Preheat the oven to 200°C (Gas Mark 6).

Lay a piece of foil 2½ times the size of the fish diagonally across an oven tray. Fold two pieces of foil into strips and place them on the foil (making 'handles' to lift the fish out).

Pour over half the olive oil and lay a third of the ginger on the foil to the length of the bass. Place the fish on the foil and stuff the cavity with the coriander and half the remaining ginger. Surround with spring onions. Pour over the remaining oils and tamari/soy sauce and cover with the remaining ginger, season with 2 tsp of sea salt and several grinds of pepper.

Wrap the 'handles' across the fish. Cut out a large piece of foil to cover the fish and make a loose parcel with edges tightly joined. Bake for 25 minutes.

Use the foil 'handles' to lift the fish on to a serving dish. Surround with the cooked spring onions. Pour the cooking liquid into a bowl and serve with the fish.

48

Lauris Morgan-Griffiths,
Hastings and Clerkenwell

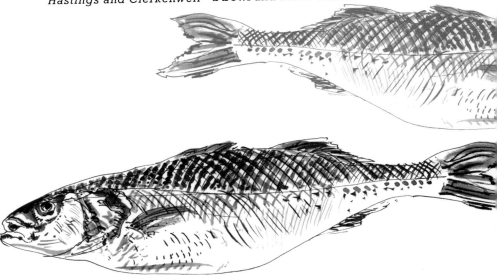

FIDEUA

4 tbsp olive oil
2 large garlic cloves
300g spaghettini broken
into 4cm pieces
Approx 225g cuttlefish
175g raw prawns
with shells
(remove shells and use
for stock)
1.5 litres home-made
fish stock, made with
fennel seeds,
½ tsp chilli flakes, prawn
shells and a slug
of dry white wine
– see page 12 for the
basic method

This is a delicious seafood pasta dish from Catalonia. When cuttlefish are available from the fishing huts, this is what I make. It does rely on a really good fish stock made from white fish heads, bones and prawn shells. I quite like the chewy texture of cuttlefish but if this isn't to your taste you can simmer it for about 40 minutes to tenderise it before making the fideua. This is adapted from Rick Stein's recipe for Catalan Noodles with Seafood, from his book Spain.

Serves 6

Place a paella or large frying pan over your largest burner. Add garlic and fry until golden, being careful not to burn it. Remove the garlic and set aside. In the same oil fry the pasta pieces till brown, stirring to avoid burning them (this would make the finished dish bitter). Stir in a litre of the fish stock, add the fried garlic, and a teaspoon of salt. Reduce to a simmer and cook gently for about 9 minutes or until the stock has been absorbed. Remove from the heat, cover with an opened out newspaper and leave to rest for 4 minutes.

Meanwhile add 2 tbsp of oil to another large frying pan and stir fry the cuttlefish and prawns over a high heat for about 2 minutes or until just cooked. Serve from the pan with the cooked seafood and a green salad dressed with olive oil and fresh lemon juice.

Elaine Partington,
Hastings

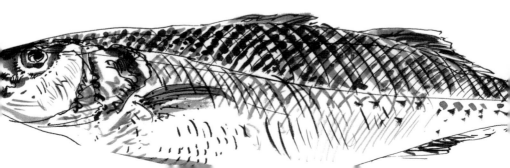

SPICY SAMBAL MACKEREL

Mackerel, gutted but left whole 3 large or 4 small shallots
4 large cloves garlic
3 large fresh red chillies
15 small or 6 large dried red chillies, soaked in hot water for at least 10 minutes
1 stalk lemongrass, chopped
1 fresh tomato
½ tsp salt (or to taste)
½ tsp sugar (or to taste)
1 tbsp rapeseed or sunflower oil

This makes more sambal than you will probably need, but you can keep it in the fridge for a couple of weeks covered in oil or freeze it for up to 3 months. If you like it spicy, this should be enough for 2-3 whole mackerel. Don't forget to wear gloves and to wash your hands thoroughly after preparing this fiery sauce.

Take all the ingredients for the sambal and grind together in a pestle and mortar. If you don't have one, just use a blender Reduce it in a pan on high heat until it becomes a loose paste with the consistency of ketchup.

Slash the mackerel 3 to 4 times on each side, about ½ cm deep. Use as much sambal as you like to coat the skin and get into the cuts. Pop it on the BBQ or under the grill for about 5 minutes each side or until the skin crisps and the eyes have gone white.

Sarah Owen,
St Leonards on Sea

Serve with basmati rice. Garnish with cucumber, lime wedges and more sambal.

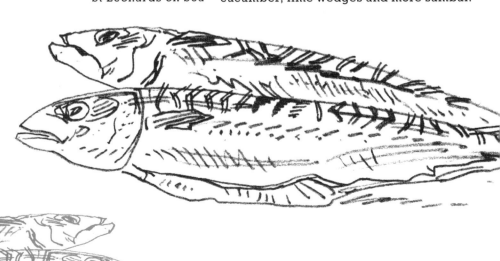

THE BEACH PAD FISH DISH

800g local white fish, filleted and cut into large chunks
1 onion, finely chopped
Pinch of saffron
2 garlic cloves, crushed
Lump of ginger, peeled and grated
2 roasted red peppers – aim for lovely large slices
2 tsp smoked paprika
Chilli to suit your taste
A handful of dried apricots or dates, halved
2 tins good quality chopped tomatoes
A punnet of proper cherry tomatoes, halved
Seasoning

For the dumplings:
4 large potatoes, chopped, boiled and mashed with their skins on (let the steam go before mashing – no need to add any milk or butter)
2 handfuls of diced black pitted olives.
To finish:
Fresh coriander or lemon wedges
Flaked almonds

Debi 'Daisy' Arnold,
St Leonards on Sea

The cooking dish is really important here. Something large and shallow will encourage the dish to reduce and give it a delicious richness. Think paella pan, rather than deep casserole dish or stock pot.

Prepare all your ingredients. Put the tinned toms, fresh toms, onion, garlic, saffron, ginger, peppers, smoked paprika, dried fruit and chilli into the pan, and leave to simmer away until beautifully reduced to an unctuous stew – about 40 minutes, depending on your dish.

51

While the stew is doing its stuff, prepare the dumplings. Once the mash has cooled, stir in the black olives and roll into little balls. Place on to a non-stick baking tray in a pre-heated oven to crisp up. While that's happening, add the fish to the stew letting it softly poach in the juices until cooked through.

Add the dumplings on top and scatter with coriander or lemon and the flaked almonds. Serve in the same dish you cooked it in.

KERALAN SEAFOOD PIE

250g peeled and de-veined raw prawns
200g smoked haddock, cut into 2.5 cm pieces
200g cleaned squid or cuttlefish, cut into strips
375g puff pastry (bought and ready rolled is fine)
1 beaten egg
2 tbsp vegetable oil
10 fresh curry leaves (available in Asian supermarkets)
1 large onion, sliced
2.5cm piece fresh ginger, peeled and sliced into fine strips
4 green chillies (small hot variety) sliced lengthways
500g fresh mussels, cleaned (discard any that do not close tightly when tapped, that are broken, or that do not open when cooked)
½ tsp ground turmeric (fresh is best if you can find it)
½ tbsp rice flour (available in Asian supermarkets)
500ml tinned coconut milk
1 tbsp black onion seeds

There is a long list of ingredients for this one, but it's well worth the effort as it is quite delicious. Serve with a small amount of steamed basmati rice and an undressed green salad, or lightly steamed whole green beans. This is adapted from Vivek Singh's recipe from Saturday Kitchen Best Bites.

Serves 4

To make the sauce heat the oil in a large frying pan. Add the curry leaves, onion, ginger and green chillies, and stir until the onion is soft but not browned. Stir in the mussels, turmeric and rice flour. Add the coconut milk and bring to a simmer, cover with a lid and cook for 2-3 minutes or until the mussels have opened and the sauce begins to turn glossy. With a slotted spoon lift out the mussels and remove them from their shells, and set them aside. Continue cooking the sauce until it thickens.

Remove the sauce from the heat and when cool, mix in the raw seafood and cooked mussels. Transfer to a 1-litre pie dish (or 4 individual ones if you prefer) placing a pie funnel in the centre. Cover with the rolled puff pastry with three slits in the centre to allow steam to escape. Knock the sides of the pastry up with a knife. Brush the pastry with the egg and sprinkle over the onion seeds.

Place on a baking tray in a pre-heated oven, and cook for 30 minutes or until the pastry has risen and is a rich brown colour. Check from time to time to ensure the edges aren't burning. (If the edges do before the centre looks cooked, cover them with tin foil).

Elaine Partington,
Hastings

LINGUINE WITH SARDINES, PINE NUTS, RAISINS & SAFFRON

Linguine – according to greed
4 sardines, scaled, gutted and filleted
Garlic clove
1 tbsp flat-leaf parsley leaves
1 dried chilli
½ tsp saffron threads or ½ tsp fennel seeds, crushed
Extra-virgin olive oil
25g pine nuts
25g raisins or sultanas
1 lemon

Serves 2

Fry the sardines on a very hot griddle pan. Sprinkle with a little salt and cook for 5 minutes. Peel and finely slice the garlic. Chop the parsley and crumble the chilli. Mash the saffron threads in a mortar, pour over three tbsp hot water and let stand for 20 minutes. Or grind the fennel seeds in a pestle and mortar.

Heat 3 tbsp of olive oil in a heavy-bottomed pan, and fry the garlic, chilli, fennel (if using) and parsley. Add the sardine fillets and fry gently for a few minutes for the flavours to meld. Season.
Brown the pine nuts in a frying pan

Cook the linguine in boiling salted water, then drain and return to the pot. Add the raisins to the pasta with the saffron and mix them together. Add the sardines and juices from the pan, and check the seasoning. Scatter over the pine nuts. Splash over some extra-virgin olive oil and lemon juice and enjoy.

Lauris Morgan-Griffiths, Hastings & Clerkenwell

THE LITTLE LARDER'S BUBBLE & SQUEAK FISHCAKES

800g potatoes
500g greens
1 onion or a leek, softened
250g peppered smoked mackerel from Rock-a-Nore Fisheries, skin off
Chives (optional)

This recipe is ever changing, depending what we have in the fridge when we make it. It is however, a firm favourite at The Little Larder and we have regulars who come in every week for them. Gluten free, and dairy free provided you don't fry the fishcakes in butter.

Makes 8
Preheat oven to 200°C (Gas Mark 6).

We start with by boiling the potatoes in salted water until tender.
Chop the greens – you can use Savoy cabbage, green cabbage, kale or even cavolo nero. Boil the greens lightly in salted water, to keep some crunch. Mash the potatoes roughly with a knife and add olive oil, plus the onion or leek. Add the greens and the chives, if you're using them.

Mix thoroughly, then turn the mixture out on to a piece of silicon paper on a baking tray and bake for 20 minutes, to dry the mixture out. Leave to cool, then add an egg and the smoked mackerel and mix well. Divide into 8 portions, shape into patties and bake for another 20 minutes.

You can either eat these straight away or chill them and warm them through late. Bubble and squeak always benefits from frying in butter and as a Northerner I prefer mine almost burnt! They also make a damn fine sandwich in buttered bread or a roll.

In the café, we serve these with a wedge of lemon and a creamy horseradish sauce. Simply mix 1 cup of crème fraîche and ½ a cup of creamed horseradish thoroughly together.

Briony Bridgmount,
The Little Larder Café,
St Leonards on Sea

HUSS BARBECUE WRAPS

For the fish:
1kg huss fillet
½ tsp each coriander and
cumin seeds, turmeric
and paprika
¼ tsp ground black pepper
¼ tsp red chilli flakes
(or fresh red chilli)
3 crushed garlic cloves
½ tsp salt
Juice of one lime
Juice of one lemon

Salsa/sambal:
450g de-seeded chopped
ripe tomatoes
½ a red onion
a garlic clove
1-2 green chillies
Juice of ½ a lemon or lime
1 tsp sugar
Chopped bunch of fresh
coriander/or mint

To finish:
Soft corn tortillas or
chapattis
Soured cream or thick
natural yoghurt
Lime or lemon wedges

Mandy Nicholl,
Hasting Old Town

56

A delicious combination of marinated fish, hot tomato salsa and cooling natural yoghurt. This recipe can have a Mexican vibe if you use corn tortillas with salsa or Indian if you go for chapattis and sambals. Either way, it's scrumptious. This recipe is very quick to prepare and cook, but the fish does need to marinate for at least 1 hour (and up to 4).

Serves 6
For the marinade, roast then grind together the coriander and cumin seeds and allow to cool before adding the ground black pepper, turmeric and paprika. Mix in the red chilli flakes or as much fresh red chilli as you fancy and 3 crushed cloves of garlic. Add a large pinch of salt. Bind together with the juice of one lemon for Indian or lime for Mexican. Mix together into a nice thick paste. Cut the fish into 12 chunks, smear the marinade over the fish and refrigerate for 1-4 hours.

For the salsa or sambal, mix together all the ingredients and chill until you are ready to serve.

When you're ready to cook, heat the grill or barbecue to hot. Cook the fish on the hot grill, turning once – about 6 minutes each side should be sufficient depending on how thick the chunks are. Warm the chapattis or tortillas in foil on the barbecue or in the oven. Place chunks of fish on the wrap, cover with the tomato mixture then a dollop of sour cream or yoghurt.
Serve with wedges of lemon or lime.

FISH PIE WITH FENNEL

500g fish fillets – flaky white fish such as cod, pollock or a mixture of the best local catch with all bones and skin removed
A large fennel bulb – choose one with fresh green fronds
3 onions
1 glass of white wine
1 bay leaf
½ a red chilli or a good pinch of dried flakes
8 black olives
Extra virgin olive oil
One tbsp plain flour

It is no coincidence that fennel bulbs are sold alongside the fish at Rock-a-Nore Fisheries – it's a marriage made in heaven. Fennel has a delicious aniseedy flavour like Pernod, which is often used instead of wine in French fish recipes. This hearty pie is strong on both flavour and looks, so is good for sharing with friends.

Serves 4 hungry people
Preheat oven to 190°C (Gas Mark 5).

Check the fish for any stray bones then chop it into generous chunks. Peel and quarter the potatoes and put on to boil. Cut off the fennel fronds and set aside, then roughly chop the bulb into wedges and add them to the potatoes after 10 minutes.
Boil for a further 10 minutes then drain, reserving the liquid.

Slice the onions thinly and fry them gently in olive oil until translucent. Sprinkle on the flour and stir while frying for a minute more. Pour in the wine and a cup of the reserved liquid then turn up the heat and boil. Stir as it thickens. Add the bay leaf and the chilli and cook for another few minutes then remove from the heat. Gently mingle the fish, olives and chopped fennel fronds with the sauce.

Oil an ovenproof dish and use half the potato and fennel on the bottom. Cover with the fish mixture then finish with the rest of the potato/fennel mixture. Drizzle with olive oil and bake uncovered for 40-50 minutes until nicely browned.
Serve with crisp green salad.

Sally Walton,
St Leonards on Sea

No mentioned!? Potatoes!!

FISH PIE WITH A FILO PASTRY

For the pie:
400g mixed fish like
gurnard and huss
(boneless)
in addition to cod
100g fresh prawns
(if you use frozen ones
make sure they
are defrosted properly)
Good handful fresh
chopped dill
5 medium carrots,
chopped
8 sheets filo pastry
50g butter
50g Cheddar cheese,
grated
Black pepper

For the béchamel:
300ml milk
2 tbsp flour
20g butter
50g Cheddar cheese
Nutmeg

Maika Crampton, Hastings

This is my mum's fish pie recipe which is complete comfort food and perfect for autumn. What makes it slightly different is the filo pastry crust. My mum used to make it with 'normal fish' like salmon and haddock, but you can easily substitute gurnard and huss for flavour. It's good to keep some cod in there for texture. Guten appetit!

Serves 4
Preheat oven to 220°C (Gas Mark 7).

Remove any skin from the fish and poach in water for 10 minutes until cooked. Drain, cool and flake into chunks. Spoon fish and prawns into a greased ovenproof dish. Blanch the carrots until slightly soft but still with a bite and drain. Mix with fish and add a good handful of chopped dill. Season.

To make the béchamel, melt the butter in a saucepan over medium heat. Add 2 tbsp plain flour, and while stirring constantly add milk slowly and bit by bit to gain a nice sauce consistency. Make up 300 ml. If the sauce is too runny, let it cook down for a while or add a little more flour. Add nutmeg and some Cheddar cheese. Pour over the fish.

Melt 50g butter and brush on to each sheet of filo pastry. Lightly scrunch, then use to top pie. Sprinkle with remaining cheese. Bake for 15-20 minutes until pastry is golden brown. Serve with steamed green veg. It'll look stunning!

DEVILLED LEFTOVERS
ON SOURDOUGH

Leftover smoked fish or
cooked and shelled
molluscs such as
mussels, winkles,
whelks or cockles
1 tbsp English mustard
1 tsp hot smoked
paprika picante
1 tsp garlic
(crushed to a purée)
2 tbsp
Worcestershire sauce
2 tbsp extra virgin
olive oil
½ tsp salt
½ tsp ground
black pepper
75ml double or
single cream
(optional –
this dish
can be enjoyed
dairy free)
1 tbsp finely
chopped parsley
(or dill)
Thick slice
of toasted
crusty bread
such as
sourdough

Andrew and Tess,
The Crown,
Hastings Old Town

This recipe is all about the sauce.
It's a super savoury umami dish.
Don't be afraid of the big flavours in the
ingredients, they combine to create a really
balanced sauce with each ingredient
complementing and mellowing the other.
We recommend this dish for lunch or as a
lighter evening meal for one. It's simple and
thrifty and you will probably have all the
ingredients stocked in your cupboard.

It's ideal for using up whatever leftover fish
you may have at home. The sauce works best
with strong flavoured ingredients such as
mussels, cockles, whelks or smoked fish
including sardines, cod, haddock, shrimp
or prawns.
We source our produce from the excellent
Rock-a-Nore Fisheries where Sonny smokes
great seafood in his shop.

In a bowl, mix the garlic, mustard, paprika,
Worcestershire sauce, salt, pepper and oil
until smooth and of uniform colour. Add your
chosen seafood to the sauce and mix until
thoroughly covered. Let the fish marinade
for a few minutes.

Heat a frying pan to a medium heat and add
the devilled fish and any remaining sauce.
As the fish or molluscs are already cooked,
you're aiming to warm the seafood through
not cook it. Once warm, take the pan off
the heat and add the cream and parsley.
Mix well.

To serve, spoon the contents of the pan over
some hot buttered sourdough toast and top
with a wedge of lemon or a side of
Hastings Lemon Ketchup.

SMOKED (AT ROCK-A-NORE) HADDOCK
with poached egg, mash, broad beans & pancetta

This is my regular nights-are-drawing-in default autumnal supper.
I always have the ingredients to hand, even if they're in the freezer
(but it's lovelier if they're fresh, obviously). The simple loveliness of
this dish comes from the yellow-on-yellow-on-yellow, as the egg yolk
oozes over the smoked fish and into the mash. I have never served
this to anything other than an accompaniment of gratifying 'mmmm!'s —
with fish dishes the simple ones are invariably the crowd pleasers.
As well as being extremely cosy, comforting and genuinely
heart-warming it's also a complete doddle – 30 minutes from start
to finish — and is best consumed with a funky glass of white and the
prospect of an evening in front of mindless Saturday night telly...

Serves 2

**2 big fillets of
smoked haddock**
2 poached eggs
**4 nice big
mashing potatoes**
400g broad beans
100g pancetta cubes
Olive oil
Butter
Milk
salt, pepper
2 lemon quarters

Preheat oven to 190°C (Gas Mark 5).
Bake the haddock, which has been dotted with a
tiny knoblet of butter and crowned with a lemon
quarter, wrapped in greased foil (oil if you're
feeling worthy, butter if you're naughty) in the
middle of the oven for 20-25 minutes,
depending on the size of your fillet.

Meanwhile, boil the potatoes, then mash them
with both butter and a few splashes of milk so
it really is super-creamy and you can make
meringue-style peaks. While the broad beans
are being either steamed or boiled, pan-fry
your pancetta cubes for a couple of minutes on
a hot flame, before stirring them into the
cooked beans.

Make a bed of mash on the plate, serve the
haddock on top of it with the beans and
pancetta to one side. Poach your eggs so they
really are ready at the very last minute —
they'll take about 5 minutes so do it while the
beans are cooking. To serve, place your egg
on top of your haddock. Ideally the egg should
be firm but still runny, so that the yolk
oozes out when you pierce it.

Kathryn Flett
Random-on-Sea

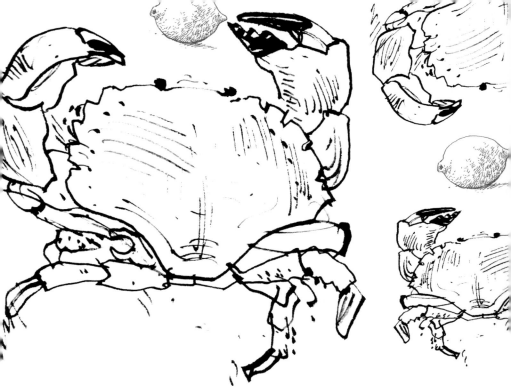

A visit to AG Hendy & Co Home Store in the High Street is like stepping into another world. Alistair is a big fan of our delicious local crabs and gave us these two recipes – one perfect for a party and the other ideal as a scrumptious quick snack.

CRAB QUICHE

1 x 375g packet ready-made shortcrust pastry
40g butter
5 small shallots, finely chopped
6 large eggs
300ml sour cream
300ml double cream
Pinch saffron stamens, warmed in 1 tbsp milk
Salt and black pepper
A good grating nutmeg or ½ tsp ground mace

Crab and egg heaven. A cress or watercress salad bound with a Dijon mustard vinaigrette makes matters perfect on serving. Eat on the day of making – refrigeration does it no favours
Serves 8 - 10

Lightly grease and base line a 23cm diameter x 5cm deep loose-bottomed metal tart tin. Roll out the pastry to the thickness of a £1 coin and use to line the tin, leaving the edges overhanging. Prick the base and bake blind in a 180°C oven (Gas Mark 4) for 15 minutes. Trim off the overhang. Turn the oven up to 190°C (Gas Mark 5).

2 large dressed crabs, brown meat separated from white Mustard cress or watercress, to serve

Gently fry shallots in the butter until translucent but not browned. Beat the eggs with the creams, saffron milk, salt and pepper, then fold in the cooked shallot and white crab meat. Mash the nutmeg into the brown meat and then spread this across the base of the pre-baked pastry case. Spoon the crab and egg mixture on top. Bake for 40 minutes, or until risen a little and pale golden brown on top.

CRAB TOAST WITH CHILLI AND LEMON MAYONNAISE

1 dressed crab
2 tbsp mayonnaise
1 tbsp chopped chives (or green part of spring onion)
½ long mild red chilli, finely chopped
1 lemon - ½ juiced, 2 quarters to serve
Sea salt and black pepper
Handful coriander leaves (thoroughly rinsed and drained)
Sourdough bread, toasted/grilled and rubbed with olive oil
Rocket and watercress, tossed with Dijon mustard dressing

Alastair Hendy
Hastings Old Town

Spread brown meat on to toast first – mix with a drop of the mayo if not spreadable. Mix mayonnaise with white meat, along with chilli, lemon juice and chives. Pile on to prepared toast, lightly season and pile loads of coriander on top.

MEDITERRANEAN SQUID
with prawns and broad beans

Serves 4
500g whole cleaned squid
or cuttlefish
250g fresh, shelled prawns
2 tbsp extra virgin olive oil
2 garlic cloves,
finely sliced
250g shelled
broad beans
1 glass dry sherry
1 glass water
1 tsp fresh,
chopped marjoram or
oregano
Salt & pepper

The true taste of the Mediterranean is right here on our doorstep with this flavour-packed recipe made from one of the best fish to be found all year in our local waters – the humble squid. Unlike some squid dishes where it's all about flash-frying and serving up instantly, the key to this dish is slow, gentle cooking to let the squid release its juices and infuse with the rich flavour of the beans.

Heat the oil gently in a large frying pan or wok. Add the garlic and let it soften, then add the squid and let it cook gently in its own juices for around 10 minutes. Then add the beans, the sherry and the water and bring to the boil before sprinkling in the seasoning and herbs. Once it's bubbling gently, turn down the heat so it's just simmering, add a lid and leave it to conjure up its magic for around 20 minutes, or until the fish is tender.

Once it's nearly done remove the lid, test your seasoning and add the prawns. Turn up the heat to evaporate some of the juices and the prawns will cook almost instantly. Don't leave it too long, otherwise they'll get floury and rather chewy.

Alastair Fairley
Hastings Old Town

Serve with a fresh green salad and some chunky organic bread to mop up the juices. **Mediterranean bliss!**

BARBECUED FISH IN NEWSPAPER

Try this with sea bass, salmon or mackerel.

I often collect charcoal on the beach from other people's leftover BBQs.

Take two pages of The Guardian. Place vine leaves (or lettuce or chard leaves) overlapping in a line the same length as your oiled and herbed fish (try fennel fronds, bay leaves or a slice or two of lime). Wrap the fish parcel firmly and tie with string. Sprinkle with enough water to dampen the paper (but not so much that the parcel falls apart) and place on the BBQ. I have a cast iron slab which I put on the grill – it distributes the heat more evenly and makes it much easier to handle a large fish. Turn the fish part way through the cooking – timing will depend on the size of the fish and the nature of the fire, but you can smell and also listen to the parcel to know when it's done! When you open the parcel, the skin comes away with the wrapping and the herbs will make the whole thing smell wonderful.

Laetitia Yhap, Hastings Old Town

MUSTARD MACKEREL

2 whole mackerel, gutted
1 or 2 tsp English mustard
1 tbsp red or white wine vinegar
2 tbsp water

My Uncle Johnny used to make this dish. It's very simple, and very, very good.

Preheat oven to 200°C (Gas Mark 6).

Score the fish, but not too deeply. Place in an ovenproof dish – you'll need to use one with a lid. Mix the other ingredients together and pour over the fish. Put the lid on and place in the oven for 30-45 minutes.

If you're feeling brave, you can whack some cayenne pepper in. Serve with a nice fresh salad and a great big hunk of fresh bread.

Mark Benton, Rye

JANE'S SKATE with caper sauce

2 small skate wings (200-250g)
1 tbsp seasoned flour
2 tbsp sunflower oil
4 anchovy fillets, drained and chopped
1 tbsp capers, drained
2 tbsp chopped parsley
2 tbsp sherry vinegar
Juice of ½ a lemon
Small piece of butter
Ground black pepper

This is a classic way to cook skate. Note that skate itself is now an endangered fish – what is usually sold under the name skate these days is actually ray, which is plentiful.

Use kitchen scissors to trim the frilly edge from the wings, dry them on kitchen paper and dredge with the seasoned flour.

Heat a non-stick pan and add the oil. When the oil starts to smoke - add the wings. Fry them until the flesh looks creamy white. Keep them warm on a serving plate.

Using the same hot pan first add the sherry vinegar which will bubble and spit then the butter, lemon juice, anchovies, capers and pepper.

Finally sprinkle on the parsley, heat through and pour over the wings.

Jane Scruton
Hastings Old Town

67

Skate wing

LOBSTER HOT DOGS

Order a
fresh lobster
to be cooked and
collected from
Rock-a-Nore.
2 tbsp good
Mayonaisse
Cayenne pepper or
Tabasco sauce
2 sticks of celery
Squeeze of lemon
Best bread rolls

Stewart Walton,
St Leonards on Sea

Hotdogs are such cheap fast-food that to mention lobster in the same breath seems ridiculous – but bear with me! I owe a big debt of gratitude to Maggie Alderson, who on noticing my food obsession, gave me a copy of Jeffrey Steingarten's book The Man Who Ate Everything. This is where I discovered the lobster hotdog that residents of Maine are all too familiar with. Hastings isn't exactly Maine but we do catch lobsters here.

This makes an expensive but unforgettable snack.

69

Break the shell with special instruments or use pliers and a hammer to extract all the meat from the tail, legs and claws. (Don't waste the shell. Crush it and boil up in water to make a great stock base.)

In a mixing bowl for each cup of lobster meat add:
2 tbsp of good mayonnaise;
A stalk or two of finely chopped celery
(this is where the crunch comes from –
not from bits of shell!).
A pinch or two of cayenne or a dash of Tabasco, a squeeze of lemon and seasoning.

Mix up being careful not to break up the lobster meat – you want a few nice chunks.

It's vital that you use very good soft rolls. Split rolls and toast under the grill till golden inside. I can't stress the importance of toasting enough. It seals the bread surface and stops it becoming soggy. Assemble and devour.

JAPANESE STYLE MACKEREL

Serves 4
4 small local mackerel,
head and tails
trimmed off
Marinade:
4 tbsp mirin sauce
3 tbsp Soy sauce
1 tbsp sake
Pepper and salt

This is mackerel marinated with mirin, soy sauce and sake and served with a crunchy, lightly pickled salad. Thai fragrant rice makes a good accompaniment.

Mix together marinade ingredients in a shallow dish. Slash mackerel diagonally along either side. Marinate mackerel for an hour, turning the fish every 15 minutes.

Salad:
Small cucumber
2 sticks celery
Small head of fennel
Handful of samphire
(if in season)
3 large spring onions
4 tbsp rice Wine
(or cider) vinegar
Handful of fresh mint

Prepare the salad while the fish is marinating. Finely chop the cucumber, celery, fennel and spring onions. Carefully wash samphire, blanch it briefly in boiling water and then plunge it in cold water and drain. Add to other ingredients.

Chop mint finely, place in small bowl and pour over 3 tbsp boiling water. Add vinegar to mint and water and season well with salt and pepper. Add vinegar mixture to salad ingredients – chill it in fridge until needed.

Heat grill. Transfer mackerel with marinade into a heatproof dish and grill for approximately 4 minutes. Turn over and grill for another 4 minutes on the other side.

Serve on a bed of rice, spooning the remaining marinade over the fish and the rice. Serve the salad alongside.

Stephanie Donaldson
Hastings Old Town

SEAFOOD TEMPURA (JAPANESE STYLE)

250ml iced fizzy water
150g SR white flour
white fish, squid, prawns
button mushrooms
red peppers
French beans,
asparagus
batons of carrot
batons of courgette

This is a great dish to serve for friends – in much the same way as a fondue used to be back in the day. It is full of excitement and drama as the selected pieces are dipped in the icy batter then dropped into hot oil where they puff up and float to the top, taking seconds to cook to a crisp. Drain the cooked pieces on kitchen paper and serve them immediately with a salty dipping sauce – vary the flavours and textures and it will be a truly memorable meal. Making the batter is very easy, but you can also now buy a readymade mix which is quite foolproof!

* You can now buy
Tempura Batter
Mixture that is
quite foolproof!

Prepare the raw ingredients by cutting everything to more or less the same size and arrange in pretty colourful piles ready to go. Whisk the batter ingredients together very lightly – lumps are fine. Don't be tempted to make the batter ahead of time – it needs to be used straight away.

Dip the assorted fish and veggies in the batter and fry in hot oil in batches. Drain the pieces on kitchen paper and eat straight away. You may need to take it in turns to fry while the other person eats. We tend to do one flavour at a time, alternating a fish with a vegetable until we cannot eat another scrap!

Stewart Walton,
St Leonards on Sea

Lovely with a soy dipping sauce. Straight from the bottle is fine but it's even better if you make your own. Put a finely grated cube of fresh ginger, 1 crushed clove of garlic, ½ a finely chopped red chilli, one tsp of sugar, 2 tbsp of rice wine or lemon juice and 3 tbsp soy sauce in pan, heat to a simmer then put aside to cool.

GRILLED SCALLOPS WITH BASIL AND LIME BUTTER

9 king scallops, shucked and cleaned
Salt and black pepper

For the butter:
85g butter, softened
2 tbsp fresh chopped basil
Juice and rind of 1 lime

Preheat the grill. If you prefer, you can remove the coral (or roe) from each scallop. Slice the scallops in half. Mix the butter ingredients together in a small bowl.

Spread half of the flavoured butter on the grill pan. Add the scallops to the pan about 5cm apart. Dot with the remaining butter and cook for 3-4 minutes, turning occasionally. Transfer to a serving dish and spoon the pan juices over them.

Serve with sliced new potatoes and salad leaves tossed in a little vinaigrette.

Paul at Arcade Fisheries,
Queen's Arcade, Hastings

DID YOU KNOW?
Unlike most fish, scallops that are too
small to sell at market can be thrown
back overboard. They float back down
to the seabed where they meet up with
other scallops. They're gregarious and
live together in large groups. Ahhh!

John Botterell of Botterells fishmongers, Rye

73

ROAST SEABASS
with salsa verde mayo

Serves 4
FOR THE FISH
1 seabass, 1.5-2kg, scaled
and gutted (or 2 smaller
fish, between 750g and
1kg each)
Lemon
Fennel seeds
Olive oil
Maldon salt

FOR THE SALSA VERDE
2 egg yolks
1 tsp Dijon mustard
Salt and pepper
Up to 300ml light olive
oil (or a mix of a neutral
oil such as sunflower or
groundnut and extra
2 cloves garlic, peeled
Six anchovy fillets
(rinsed, if packed in salt)
2 tbsp capers, rinsed
Generous handful of
parsley leaves
Generous handful of
chervil leaves (or fennel
tops, or other soft green
herb such as basil or mint)

Louise Bell,
St Leonards on Sea

Preheat oven to 200°C (Gas Mark 6). Put a few slices of lemon inside the fish, plus a generous sprinkling of fennel seeds. Season with Maldon salt, inside and out, place in a roasting dish and drizzle generously with olive oil. Roast for about 25 minutes (for a single large fish) or 15-20 minutes (for two smaller fish). Test for doneness – the fish is cooked when the flesh is opaque, but still moist, and easily comes away from the bone.

Meanwhile, make the mayonnaise. Beat together the egg yolks, mustard and salt and pepper. Gradually whisk in the oil or oils, stopping once you have a thick mayonnaise mixture. Add a generous squeeze of lemon juice. Finely chop the garlic, anchovies, capers and herbs by hand or in a food processor, and add to the mayonnaise.

Serve the fish and mayonnaise together. Puy lentils or new potatoes would be nice.

STEWART'S MUM'S BAKED FISH
with lemon mash

Serves 2
I x large or 2-3 small fillets of white fish (GURNARD/COLEY or HADDOCK)
Sliced fresh tomatoes
Mushrooms - (sliced if large)
Glass of white wine
Half a sliced lemon
Butter
Parsley
Salt and pepper

This is so easy and delicious.
Remove skin from fish and tweak out any remaining bones. Lay mushrooms in bottom of baking dish and dot with butter.
Place fish on top of mushrooms, season and dot with butter.
Place sliced lemon on top of the fish.
Arrange slices of tomato on top of fish and lemon and pour a glass of white wine over the top.
Season with more black pepper and dot with butter.
Cook at 190°C for 25 mins.
Cover with foil and bake for 15 mins.
Remove foil and bake for another 10 mins.
Serve in bowls sprinkled with chopped parsley and mashed potato flavoured with grated lemon zest.

Stewart Walton,
St Leonards on Sea

If you can't wait for mashed potato this is also nice with lots of crusty fresh bread.

QUICK KIPPER PATE

A pair of kippers
25g butter
75g full-fat cream cheese
Juice of a lemon
½ tsp horseradish
A pinch of paprika
Black pepper to taste

Ogs Storr-Hoggins, Hastings

Poach the kippers in a pan of simmering water for 8 minutes. Remove and allow to cool. Pick over the fish, removing all the skin and bones. Put the fish in a food processor with the cream cheese, lemon juice, horseradish and paprika.
Pulse to a coarse soft pâté.
Place in a suitable container, covered with clingfilm and chill until ready to eat on crusty bread or toast.

CEVICHE

**2 skinned sea bass or
lemon sole fillets
2 crushed cloves of garlic
1 red chilli, finely sliced
in rounds
1 onion, sliced into
fine rings
Juice of 2 limes
Pepper and salt**

This is a very popular way of preparing fish in South America. The fish is 'cooked' using the acidity of lime or lemon juice instead of heat. We have our friend Michael – who travelled so much in South America that we now call him Miguel – to thank for introducing it to us. We recently made this with a group of kids at a beach holiday school and they loved the magic of cooking without heat.

Place onion rings in a glass dish and cover with the fish. Cover the fish in lime juice. Sprinkle with fine sliced chilli and crushed garlic. Cover and refrigerate for 4 hours. Serve with fresh crusty bread and salad.

*Sally & Stewart Walton,
St Leonards on Sea*

78

BASQUE FISH STEW (MARMITAKO)

**Serves 4
1.5 kg of white fish fillets
try MONKFISH, COD
or COLEY
4 tbsp olive oil
1 Onion chopped
6 garlic cloves
2 red peppers
2 teaspoons paprika
¼ teaspoon of salt
¼ teaspoon of pepper
Small red chilli
6 tomatoes
(or one can of chopped
tomatoes)
1 kg potatoes
1 glass dry white wine-
Half a cup of water**

Cut the fish into 3cm chunks. Heat the oil in a heatproof casserole and saute the chopped onions, garlic and peppers, cleaned of seeds and cut into strips. When they are soft, add the tomatoes, peeled, seeded and chopped, the paprika, salt and pepper and chilli. When tomatoes are somewhat reduced add the potatoes, cut in dice.

Stir for a few minutes, then add the wine and water. Cover the pot and cook on a high heat until the potatoes are nearly tender (about 20 minutes).
Add the fish to the casserole, cover and cook another 6 minutes or until fish flakes easily but is still juicy. Take off heat for 15 minutes and let rest.

Reheat till casserole starts to bubble and remove from heat once again to sit for 5-10 minutes before serving.

*Diana J Holubowicz
St Leonards on Sea*

MARINATED MOUNT'S BAY SARDINES
with olive oil, lemon and oregano

8 sardines
3 tbsp Greek olive oil
1 tbsp lemon juice
Lamb's lettuce
Vine ripened
cherry tomatoes
Oregano

This delicious recipe is courtesy of Rick Stein, whose restaurants, writing and TV shows have done so much to raise the profile of Britain's fantastic seafood.

Serves 4

Fillet sardines, gently removing skin but leaving membrane behind. Season with salt and pepper, add lemon juice and olive oil and leave for 20 minutes.
Cut cherry tomatoes in half and mix together with the lamb's lettuce.
To serve, place lettuce and tomatoes on a plate with the sardines on top. Season and sprinkle lightly with oregano.

79

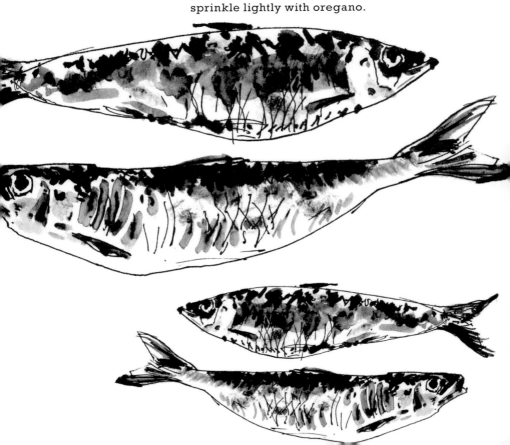

SALT-BAKED BLACK BREAM

1 large
Black Bream
(about 800g)
2 lemons or limes
Small bunch parsley
1 bulb fennel
2kg sea salt

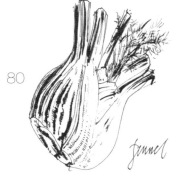

fennel

Jan Baldwin
Winchelsea Beach.

Preheat oven to 220°C (Gas Mark 7).
Clean and scale the fish but leave whole.
Stuff the fish with chopped parsley, chopped
fennel and slices of lemon or lime.

Cover the bottom of a deepish dish with sea salt
to the depth of about 3cm. Place the fish on the
salt and cover with another 3.5cm of salt. Wet
the salt well with water and pat down gently so
that a good crust forms over the fish as it cooks

Place in the hot oven. A bream of the suggested
weight will take about 15 minutes, but you will
need to adjust the cooking time depending on
the size and thickness of the fish.

When done, let the fish cool a little and then
gently remove the fish from the dish and break
away all the salt and remove the skin.
Serve with home-made mayonnaise and lemon
or lime wedges.

SMOKED MACKEREL DAUPHINOISE

400g waxy potatoes, peeled
and thinly sliced
1 large Sussex Smokers
smoked mackerel
2 bay leaves
150ml double cream
100ml milk
1 tbsp wholegrain
mustard
Salt and pepper
2 tbsp grated
Parmesan cheese
6 tbsp fresh breadcrumbs

Preheat oven to 190°C (Gas Mark 5).
Grease an ovenproof dish, and lay slices of
potato on the base, season lightly. Debone the
mackerel and cover the potato with a layer of
fish. Keep layering until the dish is nearly full.
Place the bay leaves on top. Mix the mustard
with a little of the milk, then slowly incorporate
the rest of the milk and the cream.
Pour this mixture over the fish and potato.
Mix the Parmesan with the breadcrumbs and
sprinkle evenly over the top. Cook for about an
hour. If you wish, crisp the dauphinoise under
the grill at the end of the cooking.

Sussex Smokers,
Broad Oak, Brede

'Absolutely delicious!'

THAI-STYLE SHRIMP AND COCKLE SWEET POTATO FRITTERS

150g each of brown shrimp and pre-cooked cockles
A good thumb-sized piece of fresh ginger, minced
2 tbsp sweet chilli sauce
Finely chopped spring onion
Handful of chopped coriander
1 cup each of rice flour and self-raising flour
1 cup coconut milk
A good pinch of turmeric
1 medium-sized sweet potato, peeled and grated

The local brown shrimps give a lovely subtle flavour, while the cockles add a wonderful texture to these fritters. They make a great lunch or easy supper when served with a fresh green salad.

Put the shrimp and cockles into a bowl with the ginger, chilli sauce, spring onion and coriander. Mix and allow the flavours to combine. Put both flours in a separate bowl, along with the coconut milk and turmeric. Season well. Mix to make a smooth batter. Then combine with the grated sweet potato and shrimp and cockle mix.

Heat vegetable oil in a frying pan. Drop spoonfuls of the batter into the pan and shallow fry on both sides until golden brown. Keep the fritters small and the heat medium. You'll need to cook them in several batches.

Sam Robertson,
St Leonards on Sea

Serve with wedges of lemon or lime and sweet chilli sauce.

SOUSED HERRINGS

**6 herrings,
cleaned and filleted
1 onion, sliced
60g salt**

**For the marinade:
White wine vinegar
4 bay leaves
2 tsp juniper berries
12 black peppercorns**

*Clare Gogerty,
North London on sea*

I love raw and pickled fish, especially served with rye bread, gherkins and yoghurt. Home-made rollmops are really easy to make and much more flavoursome than the commercial variety.

Dissolve salt in water to make a brine, and add the herring fillets. Leave for three hours, then drain and pat dry. Place slices of onion on each fillet. Sprinkle with juniper berries and peppercorns. Roll up, skin side out and secure with wooden cocktail sticks. Place in sterilised preserving jars (a quick wash in the dishwasher should work). Put a bay leaf in each jar. Fill to the top with white wine vinegar. Seal the jars and leave in fridge for 5 days before serving.

83

SOFT HERRING ROES
WITH CAPERS ON TOAST

6 roes per person, depending on size (of roe, not person)
Generous spoonful of capers in vinegar
Butter
Lemons
Generous handful of parsley
One thick slice of good bread per person (more if you're greedy, but the roes are quite rich)

Sally Brampton, St Leonards on Sea

Trim roes, removing green membranes or yukky bits. Chop parsley. Heat a generous knob of butter in frying pan. Bring to a good heat. Add a drop of oil to stop it burning.
Add the herring roes. Don't fry too many at once or you will steam them and end up with a mush. You want a few browned crispy edges.

As roes are cooking get the bread ready to toast.

Fry roes fast for 5 minutes, turning to make sure both sides are cooked. They will curl up so just jiggle around to make sure they cook through. Chuck in capers, along with a bit of the vinegar they are bottled in, and give one last stir before adding chopped parsley, a good squeeze of lemon and freshly ground black pepper.
Taste before adding any more salt, as the capers are quite salty.

Heap roes plus buttery juices on to toast and eat immediately. **Yum...**

SARDINES IN GINGER AND SOY SAUCE

12 sardines
1 ginger root
1 red chilli
½ cup sake
1 cup rice (or white wine) vinegar
3 tbsp mirin
2 tbsp sugar
½ cup soy sauce

Mao Bramall, Hastings Old Town

Serves 4-6
First prepare the fish (if the fishmonger hasn't already done it for you). Remove scales, cut heads off and remove guts. Wash thoroughly under running water and wipe dry.
Then cut each fish in half.

Slice the ginger very thinly and chop the chilli into small pieces.
Put the sake, mirin, vinegar and sugar in a pan large enough to hold the fish and mix well.
Add the sardines, ginger and chilli, and bring to the boil. Add the soy sauce and return to the boil. Cover the pot tightly (use foil if you don't have a lid) and simmer for 30 minutes.

DOVER SOLE
WITH NUT BROWN BUTTER.

1x 2lb Dover Sole trimmed by your fishmonger please. 25g of salted butter that has been melted in a small pan Salt and pepper to taste A sprig of flat leaf parsley Half a lemon.

Ok? Ready?
Classic Classic Classic...that all I can say about this one. Our local Dover Sole are some of the best to be found anywhere and often find themselves on the plates of some of the finest restaurants in London. This is how we do ours at the Kitchen.
Cooking anything is easy as long as you are organised. So have the ingredients and the equipment needed ready in front of you before you start.

To pan fry Seasoned plain flour 2 tablespoons of vegetable oil. A 28cm frying pan or bigger. A fish slice and an oval plate would be nice.

This will serve two.
Lightly flour the white side of the fish then brush with butter and season with salt and pepper. Heat the frying pan with the oil on a medium heat for 2 minutes. Place the fish butter side down for about 5 minutes or until you see the edges of the fish turn white and the pan juices begin to go brown. Then with the fish slice and using both hands to steady the fish, turn over back into the pan.
Cook for a further 5 minutes. Remove the fish from the pan. Add the butter, once the butter has begun to turn brown squeeze the lemon into the pan. This will froth up giving it a bubbly effect. Add the chopped parsley and then pour over that amazing Dover Sole dish you have just created

Photios Charalambous aka Fods Rock a Nore Kitchen

85

PEPPER-CRUSTED FISH IN A WARM LIME AND CORIANDER VINAIGRETTE

2 tbsp whole mixed peppercorns, coarsely crushed
2 tbsp plain flour, seasoned with salt
4 fresh cod fillets (or other white fish)
2 tbsp olive oil

For the vinaigrette:
2 cloves garlic, peeled
4 tsp mustard
Grated rind and juice of 2 limes
6 tbsp olive oil
Salt and freshly ground black pepper
Fresh coriander leaves, chopped

Alison Waters,
St Leonards on Sea

Mix together the crushed peppercorns and seasoned flour. Coat fish with the flour and peppercorn mixture, pressing well on both sides. Set aside while preparing vinaigrette.

Crush garlic into a bowl and stir in the mustard, lime rind and juice, olive oil, seasoning and coriander.

Now heat 2 tbsp olive oil in a large frying pan. Add the fish and fry for about 3 minutes on each side, until crisp and golden. Keeping the heat high, pour the vinaigrette around the fish and cook until slightly reduced.

Serve with new potatoes and greens.

Bon appétit!

Maggie's

CARIBBEAN FISH PIE

600ml goats' milk or a
dairy-free alternative
like soya or
my favorite Kara
coconut milk
(or ordinary milk)
1 sprig fresh thyme
600g local white fish
such as cod
(turbot is fab!)
55g goat's butter
(or ordinary butter)
2 tbsp rice flour,
buckwheat flour or
plain flour
50g bar of creamed
coconut
(or use the tinned type)
Salt and pepper
Juice of 1½ limes
Bunch of
fresh coriander
250g baby spinach,
kale or chard

For the mash:
900g sweet potatoes
40g goat's butter
(or ordinary butter)
Nutmeg
Allspice
Salt and pepper
*Rachel Heavens,
St Leonards on Sea*

We made this dish when we had a Caribbean-themed dinner party where we also concocted a sugar-free boozy tropical sorbet for afters. This is a super alternative to those cream- based fish pies and has the added bonus of being low GI.

Gently heat the milk in a pan with the fresh thyme and bring to the boil. Remove from the heat and leave to infuse for 30 minutes. Add the fish to the infused milk, bring up to the boil again, and remove from the heat. Remove the fish and put to one side and save the milk. Throw the thyme away and break the fish into large flakes.

Melt half the butter in a saucepan and add the flour to make a roux, then add the warm milk slowly, stirring quickly to prevent any lumps. When it starts to thicken add the creamed coconut, making sure it melts into the milky sauce. Season well with salt and pepper then add the lime juice and fresh coriander. The amount of coriander is up to you but you don't want it to overwhelm the other flavours in the dish.

Now add the spinach, which will wilt into the sauce. If you're using kale, you'll need to steam it slightly first. Add the fish last, stir gently and take off the heat.

Put the scrummy fish mixture into a dish and top with the mash.
Cook for 20-30 minutes until bubbling hot and browned on top.

87

This fishy delight is inspired by the wonderful Levi Roots' Caribbean Cooking Made Easy.

LOBSTER THERMIDOR Á LA CATHERINE

1 cooked lobster per person (ask the fishmonger to crack the shell so you can scoop out the meat easily)

2 tbsp freshly grated Parmesan Breadcrumbs for a crispy topping (finely grate a slice of very dry bread)

For the sauce:
1 tbsp Kentish cobnut oil
1 medium onion, finely chopped
250ml fish stock (buy ready-made or use a stock cube)
50ml white wine
100ml double cream
1 tsp English mustard
2 tbsp chopped parsley
Juice of ½ a lemon
Freshly ground black pepper
A few scallops (optional)

To finish:
Green beans

Catherine Robinson,
St Leonards on Sea

Remove lobster meat from the claws, tail and head. Cut into pieces and place in a bowl. Remove any unsightly bits and pieces from the shells, leaving them as clean as possible, ready to re-fill later.

For the sauce, put the cobnut oil in a pan, add the onion and cook until softened. Add the stock and wine and bring to the boil. Reduce by half. Add the double cream, mustard, herbs, lemon juice and seasoning. Mix the chopped lobster meat into the sauce to warm gently.

Put the green beans on to steam.

Pre-heat the grill. Spoon the mixed lobster meat and sauce back into the lobster halves. Sprinkle with the grated Parmesan cheese and breadcrumbs. Place the lobster halves under the grill for 3-4 minutes until golden brown – but don't burn the breadcrumbs.

If you enjoy scallops, throw these into the pan whilst the lobster is browning. Drizzle with cobnut oil, lemon juice and black pepper.

Serve with fresh green beans (drizzled with more cobnut oil!), crusty bread ...
and a glass of Champagne

KIPPER CURRY

4 kippers, filleted
3 cloves garlic, crushed.
3 tbsp vegetable oil
1 medium onion, chopped
1 tsp garam masala
½ pint milk

For the curry paste:
1 tsp ground cumin
1 tsp ground ginger
1 tsp ground coriander
1 level tsp ground chilli
1 level tsp
ground fenugreek
¼ pint hot water

Su Warren,
St Leonards on Sea

My mum used to make this for us. Delicious.

Serves 4
First mix all the paste ingredients together,
gradually adding the water.

Heat the vegetable oil in a pan, and fry the
onion and garlic until soft.
Add the spicy paste and cook for another 5
minutes. Add milk and stir over a gentle heat
until sauce thickens. Add chopped up kipper
fillets and simmer gently for another 20-25
minutes. Stir in garam masala and cook for a
further 5 minutes.

Voila! Serve with rice, chapatis and raita.

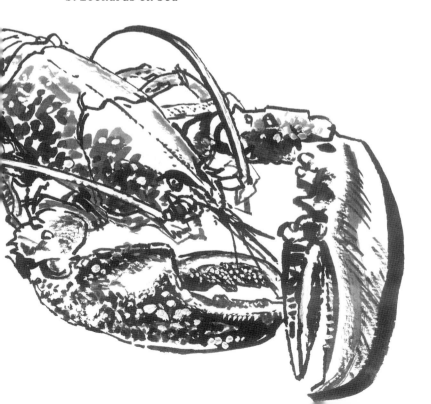

CHRISTINE'S FISHCAKES WITH SWEET CHILLI SAUCE OR LEMON MAYONNAISE

500g cod or other white fish - I go to Rock-a-Nore Fisheries and point at a piece that looks the right size
12 peppercorns
1 onion (sliced)
Milk
Bay leaf
2 medium sweet potatoes (pricked with a fork)
1 bunch of coriander, finely chopped
1 inch piece of ginger, peeled and grated on the smallest holes
1 packet of Japanese panko breadcrumbs
Vegetable oil for cooking

These are delicious, very easy to cook and inexpensive.

Makes 8-10
Set the oven to 150°C and pop in the sweet potatoes on a tray – a tray is a must as they release a toffee-like stickiness when cooking which will make a mess of your oven.

Put the cod, milk, sliced onion, peppercorns, bay leaf and milk in a large frying pan and poach the fish until cooked. Do not overcook. Remove the fish from the pan ensuring all the liquid and onion etc. has drained off, but do leave the odd peppercorn - it's a real treat for black pepper lovers to find a crunch in amongst the softness of the fishcake that bursts with that gorgeous pepper flavor. Put the fish to one side and leave to cool.

Go and have a cuppa!

Once the fish is cool, remove the skin and break the flesh up gently while searching for bones. Don't mash – you're aiming for nice small flakes. Do go through the flaked fish one more time checking for bones.

Potatoes cooked? They should be very soft. Remove from the oven, slit them down the middle and leave to cool then scoop the flesh from the skin with a spoon, put into a separate bowl and mash. Finely chop the coriander, then put some breadcrumbs in a shallow bowl ready for coating the fishcakes.

Now to combine. Add the fish to the mashed sweet potato, gently with your hands then add as much coriander as you like

Deeeelicious

(the mixture should be quite green) and the grated ginger. Gather into burger-sized fishcakes. The mixture will be moist, but don't worry. Coat each fishcake with the breadcrumbs and voila! Your fishcakes are ready to fry in light vegetable oil.

Deeeelicious served with salad and either a sweet Thai chilli sauce or lemon mayonnaise. To make the lemon mayonnaise, combine 4 tbsp mayonnaise with ½ tbsp grainy mustard and the juice of half a lemon – feel free to add more of both! Serve in a separate small bowl alongside the fishcakes.

Christine Shepherd, Hastings

91

BAKED OMELETTE WITH SMOKED FISH FROM BORNHOLM (BORNHOLMSK ÆGGEKAGE MED RØGET FISK)

5 eggs
150g local hot smoked salmon or smoked mackerel
100ml milk and cream mixture
1 shallot, finely chopped
2 boiled potatoes, cubed
Salt and pepper to taste
Plenty of chopped chives

Lone Ormonde, Hastings

Great for lunch or a light dinner.
Serves 2

Preheat oven to 180°C (Gas Mark 4).

Whisk egg, milk and cream together. Add freshly ground pepper and salt. Pour mixture into a greased ovenproof dish. Add the cubed potatoes and finely chopped shallot to mixture. Bake for about 15 minutes, or until mixture has thickened but not set.

Break up the smoked fish into smaller pieces and arrange them on top, so they are just partly submerged in the mixture. Bake for another 15 minutes or until mixture has set. Keep an eye on it – you don't want it to overcook. Sprinkle with chopped chives and serve Danish-style with tomato salad, rye bread and a cold beer.

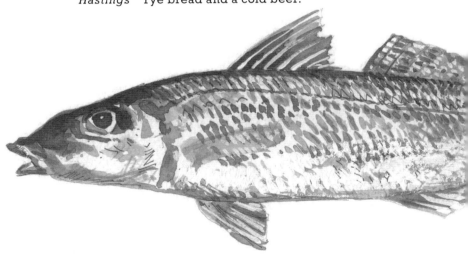

HERB-CRUSTED WHITING ON CREAMY SAUERKRAUT

4 fillets of local whiting
1 egg yolk
1 tsp English mustard
1 large clove of garlic
3 slices of white bread
Chopped parsley,
chives and thyme
(a small teacup full)
About 450g sauerkraut
(canned or bottled –
rinse well before using)
1 cup white wine
1 large onion
100ml double cream
2 tbsp paprika
2 bay leaves
2 cloves
3-4 juniper berries,
gently crushed

Fry the chopped onion until soft and translucent, then add the rinsed sauerkraut, wine and spices and cook for approximately 20 minutes with the lid on.

In the meantime, take the crusts off the bread and discard. Chop the rest of the bread coarsely and put it into a blender. Blend until flaky, then add the herbs and mix gently.

Blend the egg yolk with mustard and the finely chopped garlic.

When the sauerkraut is cooked, add the paprika and stir in the double cream. Cook for another minute or two or longer if needed to reduce the liquid. The sauce shouldn't be too runny.

Preheat the grill of your oven to its highest setting.

Put the flour-dusted fillets in a large frying pan with hot sunflower oil and fry for a minute or two on each side (depending on their size). Take them out, season with salt and pepper and place on an ovenproof tray. Now you need to move fast! Baste the top side with the egg yolk and carefully heap the breadcrumb-herb mixture on to the fish. Press gently.

Put the fish under the grill and cook until golden. This should only take a minute or two. In the meantime, arrange the sauerkraut in the middle of the dishes.

Florian Schüßler,
Pett Level and Berlin

Place the fillets on top of it.

GOAN SHRIMP MASALA

200g shrimps
1 onion,
finely chopped
2 cloves garlic,
finely chopped
Coriander seeds
Cumin seeds
or powder
Fenugreek seeds
(optional)
Turmeric
Fresh coriander
Red lentils
1 inch root ginger
Packet of
creamed coconut
Juice of ½ a lemon

Rose Ratcliffe,
Hastings Old Town

Serves 2 or 3 greedy people

Dry fry a tablespoon of coriander, cumin and fenugreek seeds for a couple of minutes, tossing the pan so they don't burn. Add some oil, then the onion, garlic, half a bunch of fresh coriander (finely chopped), the grated root ginger and a little turmeric for colour. Fry gently, keeping the heat low, until the onion is soft.

Meanwhile, cook 100g of orange lentils in boiling water for about five minutes, then drain. Add the peeled shrimps and lentils to your masala fry. Add ¼ of the packet of creamed coconut and a ¼ pint of water on a gentle heat until it all starts to look and smell delicious. Squeeze half a lemon into it then serve with basmati rice.

It's even better left overnight and reheated the next day.

BARBECUED SESAME SQUID WITH ASIAN SALSA

Fresh squid – your fishmonger will be able to clean it for you, but it's easy to do if you fancy having a go yourself.
½ cup sesame seeds

For the salsa:
A large bunch of coriander
Fresh chilli
1-2 cloves of garlic
A thumb-sized piece of peeled ginger
2 anchovies
Lemon or lime juice
Salt and pepper

Sam Robertson, St Leonards on Sea

Being a Kiwi, barbecuing is never far from my mind. This squid is easy, fast and borrows some great south-east Asian flavours. Squid is at its best cooked really fast, so don't spare the heat.

To make the salsa, put the whole bunch of coriander – stalks and all – into a food processor along with the garlic, ginger, chilli (leave the seeds in if you like a bit of a kick), anchovies and a good squeeze of lemon or lime. Add a little olive oil and season. Blitz to a fine salsa. This can be done well ahead of time and will keep in the fridge for several days.

Cut the squid into large pieces – be warned, if they're too small they'll fall through the grill. Use a knife to score the squid lightly, making a diamond pattern on one side. I tend to leave the tentacles whole – don't be squeamish about these, they're arguably the best bit. Season well. Toss over the sesame seeds ensuring light but even coverage – you aren't trying to crumb them. Drizzle over a little oil to stop the squid sticking to the grill. Cook on a fierce heat for about 90 seconds, turning once.

Serve immediately with the salsa.

BAKED BASS OR GREY MULLET

2kg sea bass or grey mullet, filleted
Fennel bulb
2 large tomatoes
1 medium onion, finely sliced
Salt and pepper
Oil

In this 'sandwich' with an onion, fennel and tomato filling, the bread is replaced with lovely fresh fillets of fish. Both bass and grey mullet are caught off Hastings – *just ask for what's best on the day.* Slice the fennel bulb quite finely lengthways. Slice the onion into fine rings. Cut the tomatoes into thicker slices. Place one seasoned fillet on an oiled baking tray and arrange the fennel, onion and tomato slices across it. Now place the other seasoned fillet on top to make the sandwich.

96

Sonny,
Rock-a-Nore Fisheries

Bake in a hot oven for 20 minutes and serve with whatever you like – salad, potatoes or steamed broccoli.

BAKED COD WITH CHERRY TOMATOES

Fillet of cod
Milk
Breadcrumbs
Butter
Cheese
Cherry tomatoes

Gail,
Rock-a-Nore Fisheries

An easy dish to pop in the oven. Add crusty bread and a green salad, and you've got dinner in 30 minutes. Adjust the amounts depending on whether you're feeding one or a crowd!

Dip the cod in milk, then breadcrumbs. Put in an oven dish with cherry tomatoes. Cover with melted butter, sprinkle over some grated cheese and bake for 25 minutes.

MONKFISH BAKED WITH BACON

**1kg monkfish
(ask the fishmonger
to skin it,
but not fillet it)
2 onions
125g streaky bacon
4 tomatoes
50g butter
150ml dry white wine**

Preheat oven to 180°C (Gas Mark 4).

Chop onions, bacon and tomatoes into small pieces. Cook onions in butter then add bacon and tomatoes and cook till they are soft. Place half the mixture into an oval fireproof dish which has been lightly buttered. Put the fish on top, then cover with the remaining mixture. Pour the wine over the fish.

Cover with buttered foil and place in the oven for about 50 minutes or until fish is opaque but still moist inside.

*Candy Upton,
St Leonards on Sea*

Serve with a nice leafy salad and new potatoes

...and a raised glass of Prosecco in Candy's memory

MARIA'S COD WRAPPED IN HAM

6 cod fillets
75g unsalted butter
6 slices Parma ham

I love this old Italian recipe as it's SO quick and I am SO impatient! I like to serve this with red quinoa as the colours look nice.

Preheat oven to 200°C (Gas 6).

Brush the fish with melted butter. Wrap in the ham (if you're getting it sliced specially, ask for slightly thicker slices) then brush with butter again.

Maria McErlane
St Leonards on Sea

Pop on a non-stick baking tray and into the oven for 15 minutes. Yum!

'I like to serve this with red quinoa as the colours look nic
You can also add dried cherries and pecan nuts to the quin
if you wish to be really exotic!'

THAI-STYLE MACKEREL

4 mackerel
1 lemon
2 limes
Extra virgin olive oil
Sesame oil
1 red chilli
Handful of fresh coriander
Couple of sprigs of fresh mint
Soy sauce
Ginger
Honey
Spring onion
Sea salt and black pepper

*Tara Reddy,
St Leonards on Sea*

Sprinkle some sea salt, black pepper and lemon zest over your mackerel and grill for about 8 minutes.

Meanwhile make the scrummy sauce. Grate the garlic and ginger and finely chop the spring onion and chilli, add lemon and lime zest and their juices, add the olive oil, sesame oil, soy sauce and honey and mix it all up. The fish should be ready now.

Pop it on the plate and pour over the sauce, then sprinkle over the coriander and mint.
Serve with rice and enjoy!

FILETS DE GURNARD

**As many fillets per person as seems appropriate (gurnards vary wildly in size)
Breadcrumbs (using crumbs from a mix of different loaves adds to the interest)
Olive oil
A lemon
About 1 tbsp capers, if you like them**

Gurnard is the ugliest fish with the sweetest taste, but the supply of this splendid critter is quite variable, so you can make this with pretty much any other non-oily fish fillet.

Serves 2
Heat oven to 180° (160° if fan) (Gas Mark 4).

Place the fillets in a ceramic baking dish you have pre-drizzled with olive oil and drizzle a bit more over the fish.

Mix a couple of handfuls of breadcrumbs with the zest of half the lemon. Pack it over the top of the fillets, pressing it on to a thickness of about ½ cm. Squeeze the juice of the lemon over the top, so that the breadcrumbs stick together. If you like capers, press them into the crust now. You can also add chopped parsley. Sprinkle over pepper and sea salt and bake in the oven.

Have a look after 10 minutes, poking with a sharp knife to see if the fish is cooked through. If it isn't, give it another 5 minutes.

Maggie Alderson, Hastings Old Town

I usually serve this with brown basmati rice and green beans.

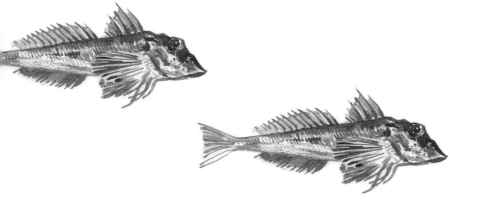

ZESTY COD

2 x 200g cod fillets (or use haddock, whiting or pollock)
1 heaped tbsp whole black peppercorns, crushed coarsely
1 heaped tbsp plain flour, seasoned with a little salt
1 tbsp olive oil

Here's my fave, yummy, easy fish dish. Cod caught off Hastings is so sweet and delicious. For me, nothing beats it – but of course you can use another light white fish if you prefer.

Serves 2
Mix the flour and crushed peppercorns on a plate. Remove skin from fish and dry on kitchen paper, then press the fish into the flour mix covering well on both sides.

For the vinaigrette:
3 cloves garlic (grated on a JR clay garlic grater!)
2 tsp coarse or Dijon mustard
Juice of 2 limes (plus grated zest if you like)
4 tbsp olive oil
Sea salt and freshly ground black pepper
Handful of coriander or parsley, chopped

Prepare the vinaigrette. Grate the garlic, put it into a bowl and stir in the mustard, lime juice and zest, olive oil, salt, pepper and herbs.

Heat a tablespoon of olive oil in a large frying pan. When hot, add the fish and fry on each side until crispy and golden. Keeping the heat high, pour in the vinaigrette around the fish and maintain heat to reduce a little for 5 minutes.

Serve with potatoes and green beans or crusty bread and green salad.

Judith Rowe, Hastings

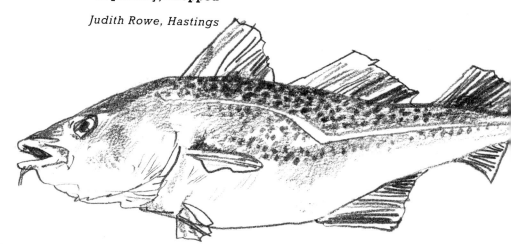

SQUID AND CHICKPEAS WITH RED PEPPERS, FRESH HERBS, CHILLI AND GARLIC

**6 small or
3 medium squid
2 red peppers
3 cloves of garlic
Bunch of parsley
½ bunch of coriander
1 red chilli chopped,
with seeds removed if
you're sensitive
Olive oil
½ glass white wine
Tin of chickpeas
(use less if you like)
Salt and black pepper**

This is the kind of thrown-together, visually stunning, rustic dish that completely blows everyone away. A bit of prep will mean you can produce it in minutes and delight the famished. It's a(nother) very good reason to live in Hastings, where squid is so fresh and plentiful. The only accompaniment needed is fresh bread and a chilled bottle of beer or wine.

Serves 4
Roast the red peppers by turning them over a gas ring or in the oven until the skin turns black. Pop them in a plastic bag to sweat for 20 minutes, then rub the skin off and pull out the seedy stems.

Next, clean the squid. You can ask the fishmonger to do this for you – but I enjoy it!
Cut off and keep the tentacles. Cut off the head, then pull the glassy spine and any 'insides' out of the body and rub off the darker skin. Note that the bits swiftly turn smelly, so wrap them up in newspaper and put them in the outside bin.

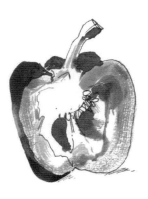

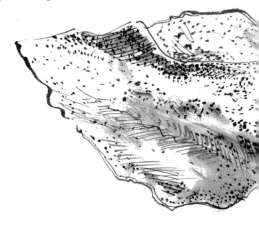

You can do this in
advance and leave the
squid in a dish of soda
water or water with
tsp bicarb.
This will prevent it
om turning rubbery
hen cooked.

Wash the squid body and tentacles under the
cold tap, then open up the body to create a
rectangle. Score this lightly, then cut into 5cm
squares. Chop the tentacles to the same length.

Cut the red pepper into narrow strips and crush
the garlic, chop the chilli and herbs so that
everything's ready to go. Put 2 tbsp of herbs
aside to sprinkle when serving.

Heat a heavy pan and add a good splash of olive
oil. Fry the garlic, salt and pepper, coriander
and parsley gently for 2 minutes. Add the
chopped red pepper and chilli and fry for
2 minutes. Turn up the heat, add the squid and
fry for 2 minutes on each side. Add the wine and
stir to coat the squid. Tip the chickpeas in and
stir it all together over the heat for another 2
minutes.

103

Sally Walton,
St Leonards on Sea

Remove from heat and serve sprinkled with the
remaining chopped herbs.

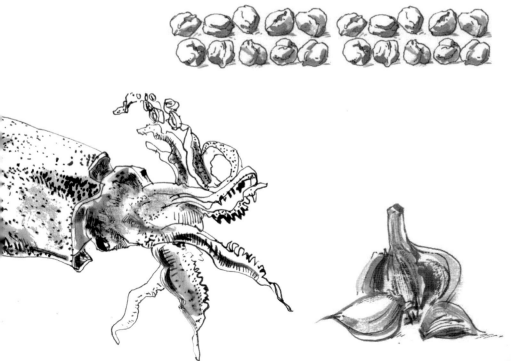

SKATE WITH ROASTED CHERRY TOMATOES

400g vine-ripened cherry tomatoes
Olive oil
4 x 300g skate wings
Sea salt and pepper
½ tsp dried red chilli flakes
1 lemon, quartered, for serving
For the dressing:
2 tbsp extra virgin olive oil
1 tbsp lemon juice
1 tsp Dijon mustard
1 tbsp salted capers, rinsed
Sea salt and pepper

Stephanie Donaldson, Hastings Old Town

This is a delicious recipe that doesn't involve butter.
It was devised by the wonderful Australian chef Jill Dupleix.

Serves 4
Preheat oven to 180°C (Gas Mark 4). Coat the cherry tomatoes in 1 tbsp of olive oil and roast in a large roasting pan for 10 minutes.

Season the skate wings with salt and pepper and a pinch of dried chilli. Heat a little extra olive oil in a pan and lightly brown the skate on the top side.

Transfer to the roasting pan, moving the tomatoes to one side, and roast for a further 10-15 minutes (depending on the size of the wings) or until the meat lifts away easily from the cartilage.

For the dressing, whisk the olive oil, lemon juice, mustard, capers, sea salt and pepper in a bowl. Add the roast tomatoes and lightly crush until they burst. Spoon the tomatoes and their juices over the top of each skate wing.
Serve with lemon quarters.

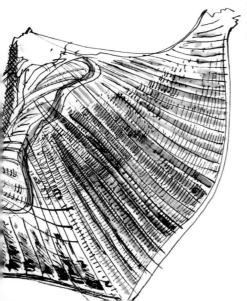

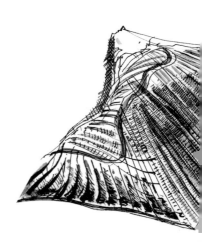

PLAICE ESCAB-ISH

4 large plaice fillets
Olive oil
1 shallot, finely sliced
2 garlic cloves,
finely sliced
1 bay leaf
Pinch saffron
1 tsp coriander seeds
1 tsp cumin seeds
½ tsp black peppercorns
(or pink, if you
have them)
Scant pinch chilli flakes
100ml dry white wine
50ml white wine vinegar
Pinch sugar
Plain flour seasoned with
salt and black pepper,
to dust

Escabeche is a way of gently pickling fish. Rather than tasting vinegary, it should be aromatic and gently tangy – perfect with the sweet, earthy flavour of Hastings' very own sustainably-caught plaice. This recipe is easily scaled up, and is also great made with oily fish such as mackerel.

Serves 2 for lunch or supper,
or 4 as a starter

Heat a tablespoon of oil in a heavy pan and gently fry the shallot until soft but not coloured. Add the garlic, herbs and spices and cook gently for a couple more minutes. Add the wine, vinegar and sugar, and simmer for 10 minutes.

While the marinade is simmering, dip the plaice in the seasoned flour and fry gently in more olive oil until just cooked. Pour the hot marinade over the fish and allow to cool. This is best left for a few hours before eating, to allow the flavours to permeate the fish.

Serve with toasted country bread, rubbed with garlic and drizzled with good olive oil, or turn it into a substantial salad by mixing chunks of the fish with cooked white beans, a few stoned black olives, a pinch of smoked paprika and plenty of chopped parsley.

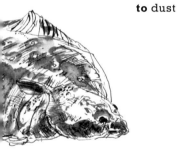

Louise Bell,
St Leonards on Sea

NANCY'S VEGETABLE AND CHIC-PEA STEW

**6 portions of chunky fish
with not too many bones
(try haddock, coley or huss)
1 onion, finely chopped
2 carrots,
chopped into 1cm pieces
2 tsp smoked paprika
About ½ tsp chilli flakes,
depending on whether
you like it hot
1 tin tomatoes
6 sundried tomatoes
1 tin chickpeas
1 red pepper, chopped
2 medium courgettes,
chopped into 2cm chunks
2 cloves garlic, crushed
A handful of parsley,
chopped
1 pint stock
White wine (optional)
Oil**

*Nancy Roche,
St Leonards on Sea
and Brixton*

You will need a deep pan or casserole dish with a lid. This is the pot you are serving the stew in, so choose something dramatic, especially if you have guests. If courgettes and peppers aren't available, use whatever's in season – green beans and sweet potatoes are both great.

Fry the onions and carrots until soft, add garlic and cook for 2 minutes, add the peppers and courgettes and allow them to sweat. Add the sundried tomatoes, smoked paprika and chilli flakes and continue to cook, stirring, for about 10 minutes. Add the tinned tomatoes (chopped up), parsley and chickpeas. Cook for a while, then add the stock and a glass of white wine. Stir occasionally.

Increase the heat, and simmer until the liquid is reduced and you have a thickish stew. 20 minutes should be sufficient. Taste, and season with salt and pepper.

At this point, part one is ready. Now reduce the heat to a very gentle simmer and add the fish. Cover with the lid and leave to cook. It should be ready in about 7 minutes, depending on the thickness of the fish.

Serve with brown rice.

SALT COD FRITTERS WITH PARSLEY AND GARLIC

500g dried salt cod fillets
1 fresh bay leaf
2 medium-sized floury potatoes, peeled and thinly sliced
Olive oil
50g plain flour
3 medium eggs
garlic cloves, crushed
2 large sprigs flatleaf parsley (leaves only)
Salt and pepper
Aioli (homemade is best)

If you look up in any good fishmongers you may see a few cuts of fish dangling down from the ceiling like nicotine-stained laundry. Salt cod is an acquired taste. Given enough time, salt dries out any moisture from the fish and sets it into solid form. Salt cod can last for months, but takes only 24 hours of soaking to bring back to life. At St Clements we salt our own fish for just 48 hours. It's a subtler way of salting that adds firmness and flavour but doesn't give that 'fishy', slightly woolly, texture that can put people off. This is a really nice light lunch to eat in the garden and the good news is that preserving fish in this way makes the flavour robust enough to withstand a beer or two.

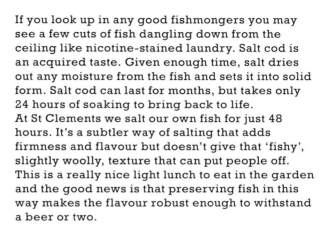

Rinse off any excess salt from the cod and soak in cold water in the fridge for 36-48 hours. You will need to change the water 3-4 times a day. When you are happy with the level of saltiness, drain and cut into small pieces then put into a pan of water with the bay leaf. Bring to just below boiling point, then remove from the heat and leave to stand for 10 minutes. Take the fish out of the water (don't throw the water away), allow to cool, then flake, getting rid of any skin or bones. Put the potatoes in the water you used to poach the fish and boil for 10 minutes until tender.

In a separate pan bring 300ml of water and 2 tbsp olive oil to the boil. Remove from the heat and gradually beat in the flour to form a batter. Cool slightly, then beat in the eggs one at a time.

St. Clement's

Mash the potatoes and mix in a large bowl with the salt cod, garlic and parsley. Season. Then combine the cod mixture with the batter and cook on a low heat for 10 minutes or until you reach the consistency of mashed potatoes. While it cools, heat some oil for deep frying to 190°C. Roll the batter mixture into 20 small balls and fry in batches of 5 for 3 minutes per batch. Serve with aioli.

Nick Hales,
St Clements Restaurant,
St Leonards on Sea

MACKEREL TARTARE

1 fresh mackerel
½ a shallot, finely chopped
1 tsp chives, finely chopped
2 tsp light soy sauce
1 tsp rice vinegar
Crème fraiche
1 tsp olive oil
2 cooked beetroot,
thinly sliced
(use a mandolin if possible)

Paul Webbe,
Webbe's Rock-a-Nore

Serves 2
Skin and fillet the mackerel. Finely chop the flesh. Add chopped shallots, chives, soy sauce and vinegar. Add salt and pepper to taste.
Press into a ring.

Place the mackerel on a plate and remove ring. Fan the sliced beetroot on top and finish with crème fraiche.

RYE BAY SCALLOP CEVICHE

500g Rye Bay scallops
cut into quarters
(I like to use the orange roe,
but you can leave it out
if you prefer)
2 large tomatoes, chopped
1 red onion, chopped finely
½ a jalapeno pepper,
chopped finely
1½ limes, juiced
½ cup orange juice
3 tbsp chopped coriander
Salt and pepper to taste

Alexa Haywood, Hastings

Mix all the ingredients together and allow to marinate for 3-4 hours. The citrus juices will cook the fish.

Top with avocado and a sprinkle of coriander, and serve with tortilla chips and a cold beer!

SOUTH INDIAN-STYLE DEEP-FRIED FISH

5g chilli powder
1 chopped chilli
1 sprig coriander leaves
1 sprig mint leaves
10g coriander powder
10g rice flour
5g plain flour
3g garam masala
1 sprig fresh curry leaves
4 fillets of fish, cut into
large cubes
10g ginger garlic paste
5 tsp lemon juice
1 pinch turmeric
Salt to taste
Oil for deep frying

For the garnish:
1 lemon, sliced
2 onions, sliced
Marinate fish
with all the ingredients
and fry on a medium heat
on both sides.
Garnish with lemon
and onion.

Lakshmi (head chef)
Lakshmi Mahal,
St Leonards on Sea

The Taj Mahal restaurant – now the Lakshmi Mahal – in St Leonards on Sea opened quietly in 2010 but it didn't take long for the word to get round. It's special because the style is South Indian and everything is freshly prepared. Diners watch the cooking through the large window into the kitchen and the talented chef is a lady

Marinate fish with all the ingredients and fry on a medium heat on both sides. Garnish with lemon and onion.

VIC REEVES MUSHY PEA FISH PIE

500g catch of the day fillets and a piece of hot smoked salmon

Mushy peas

Butter

Milk

Plain flour

Bay leaf

Chopped parsley

500g floury potatoes, peeled and cut in half

Toasted breadcrumbs

Extra butter for dotting

Salt and pepper

Vic Reeves, artist & comedian, 10 miles east of Rye

Sally Walton writes: When we began collecting fish recipes, a trend quickly emerged – fish pie. Everyone loves it, and we included a classic version in Book 1. Since then, we've been on the look-out for something different, hence the delicious-sounding Caribbean version with sweet potato mash and coconut milk on page 87. After that, the message to contributors was: anything, as long as it's not fish pie.

That was before we met Vic Reeves at a friend's party. After the briefest of introductions, we asked did he like to cook fish and how about a recipe for the book? He replied that he made a really good fish pie. Damn. Then he revealed the secret ingredient and we were completely bowled over by its brilliance. So simple, so right.

Preheat oven to 180°C (Gas Mark 4). Put a large pan of water on to boil and add the peeled chopped potatoes.

Tip the two tins of mushy peas into the bottom of an ovenproof dish. Season with salt and pepper.

Poach the fish lightly in milk, adding the bay leaf, then strain, reserving the milk for the béchamel. Pull the fish apart gently into chunky flakes.

Make the sauce by melting a knob of butter, mixing in a dessertspoon of flour and stirring for a couple of minutes until it's foamy. Then pour in the milk, discarding the bay leaf, stirring all the time to a nice smooth creamy consistency. Chopped parsley can be added at this stage. Season well and fold in the fish. Spoon the fish layer over the mushy peas.

The potatoes should be ready by now so strain and mash them with butter, and a splash of cream or milk if you like. Potatoes mashed in the pan over a low heat are very light and creamy. Season and spread the potatoes over the fish.

Sprinkle breadcrumbs on the top – nice mixed with parsley – dot with butter and for 30 minutes or until the top has browned.

FARMERS' MARKETS

HASTINGS FARMERS' MARKET - TOWN CENTRE
2nd and 4th Thursday of the month

EAST SUSSEX & KENT FARMERS' MARKETS WITH A FRESH FISH STALL
Advanced orders can be placed with **BOTTERELLS** 01797 222875
RYE Wednesdays 10am-midday
ROLVENDEN Thursdays 10am-midday
BREDE Fridays 10am-midday
BATTLE 3rd Saturday 9am-1pm
& **ARCADE FISHERIES** 01424 435459
PENSHURST PLACE 1st Saturday of the month 9.30am-midday
THE PANTILES - TUNBRIDGE WELLS
3rd Saturday of the month 9am-midday
SHOREHAM 2nd Saturday of the month 9am-2pm
TOWN HALL SQUARE TUNBRIDGE WELLS - KENT
4th Saturday of the month 9am-2pm
HIGH STREET WEST MALLING - KENT
4th Sunday of the month 9.30am-1.30pm
AYLESFORD PRIORY - KENT
3rd Sunday of the month 9am-1.30pm

ANNUAL FOODIE EVENTS

**THE MIDSUMMER FISH FESTIVAL is held at the Stade,
Hastings Old Town, in JUNE.**
Check dates at www.hastingsflag.org

**THE HASTINGS SEAFOOD & WINE FESTIVAL is held
at the Stade, Hastings Old Town, in MID-SEPTEMBER.**
Check dates at www.visit1066country.com

**THE HASTINGS HERRING FAIR is held at the Stade
in Hastings Old Town in early NOVEMBER.**
Check dates at www.visit1066country.com

**RYE SCALLOP WEEK is celebrated in FEBRUARY
with scallop-related events, cooking demonstrations,
special restaurant menus and a cookery school.**
Check dates at www.ryebayscallops.co.uk

SLOW FOOD SUSSEX

At Slow Food we believe that food is one of life's great pleasures and that it should be, in the words of Slow Food's founder Carlo Petrini : "Good, clean and fair".

With this in mind we seek out local artisan producers of good food and drink as well as those further afield and learn more about the traditions of quality and good taste that go into producing real, natural foods.

We share good food experiences and events such as learning to bake bread; apple picking and pressing and visits to local dairies. We connect with local growers, share pot-luck suppers and organise weekend morning brunches to be enjoyed with fellow food lovers.
You can join Slow Food nationally www.slowfood.org.uk but membership is not necessary to attend local events. Make contact via the national website.

EATING THE LOCAL CATCH AROUND HASTINGS & RYE

ST CLEMENTS
Top chef and great food with
daily fish specials
3 Mercatoria
ST LEONARDS ON SEA
01424 200355

**AG HENDY & CO
HOMESTORE**
Freshly cooked local fish
36 High Street
HASTINGS OLD TOWN
TN34 3ER
01424 447171
Open: Thurs-Sun
homestore-hastings.co.uk

SMITHS REAL FOOD
Great daytime food
21 Grand Parade
ST LEONARDS ON SEA

PIER NINE
Beautiful surroundings
and great menu
Zanzibar Boutique Hotel
9 Eversfield Place
ST LEONARDS ON SEA
01424 460109

WEBBE'S ROCK-A-NORE
Fabulous seafood in
contemporary style
with tasting bar and
outdoor terrace opposite
the fishing beach
1 Rock-a-Nore Road
HASTINGS OLD TOWN
01424 721650

LAKSHMI MAHAL
Authentic southern
Indian restaurant
Western Road
ST LEONARDS ON SEA
01424 200 355

THE ROCK-A-NORE KITCHEN
Modern British with a
'catch of the day'
27a Rock-a-Nore Road
(opp. Fishermen's Museum)
HASTING OLD TOWN
TN34 3DW
01424 433764

THE CROWN
Eating the local catch
around Hastings & Rye
64-66 All Saints St.
HASTINGS OLD TOWN
TN34 3BN
01424 465100
thecrownhastings.co.uk

THE DRAGON BAR
Established cool bar
with really great food
George Street
HASTINGS OLD TOWN
01424 423688

THE SHIP
Restaurant, bar, deli
and butchers
with a fabulous
coastal-themed garden
Sea Rd
WINCHELSEA BEACH
TN36 4LH
01797 226767

WEBBE'S AT THE FISH CAFÉ
Brasserie specialising
in delicious fish
17 Tower St
RYE
01797 222226

THE GALLIVANT
Beach-vibe hotel with
great restaurant specialising
in locally sourced produce
New Lydd Road,
Camber Sands
RYE
01797 225 057

THE FISHMONGERS

ROCK-A-NORE FISHERIES
Fresh fish, oysters
and smokery
3 Rock-a-Nore Road
HASTINGS OLD TOWN
TN34 3DW
01424 445425
rockanore.co.uk

ARCADE FISHERIES
Fresh fish daily
in the town centre
13 Queen's Arcade
HASTINGS
TN34 1TA
01424 435459
arcadefisherieshastings.co.uk

**PETER'S EASTERN
FISH SHOP**
Fresh fish daily
Rock-a-Nore Road
HASTINGS OLD TOWN
01424 422342

RX FISHERIES
Fresh fish daily
Rock-a-Nore Road
HASTINGS OLD TOWN
TN34 3DW
01424 445239

RYE BAY FISH
Fresh fish from the
Rye fleet
73 New Road (by the bridge)
RYE
TN31 7LS
01797 222377

SUTTONS FISH SHOP
Quality provisions and fresh fish
daily
Sea Road
WINCHELSEA
East Sussex
TN36 4LA

BREAD
AND OTHER PROVISIONS

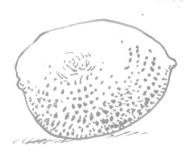

JUDGE'S BAKERY
Organic bread and
provisions store
51 High Street
HASTINGS OLD TOWN
TN34 3EN
01424 722588

TRINITY WHOLEFOODS
Good for herbs and spices,
fresh organic veggies
and lots more
3 Trinity Street
HASTINGS
TN34 1HG
01424 430473

THE SHIP
Provisions, deli counter
and wine, plus meat
from butcher Jamie Wickens
Sea Road
WINCHELSEA BEACH
TN36 4LH
shipwinchelseabeach.com

THE OAK BAKERY
Excellent sourdough
baked Monday to Saturday
17 London Road
ST LEONARDS ON SEA
TN37 6AJ
01424 435966

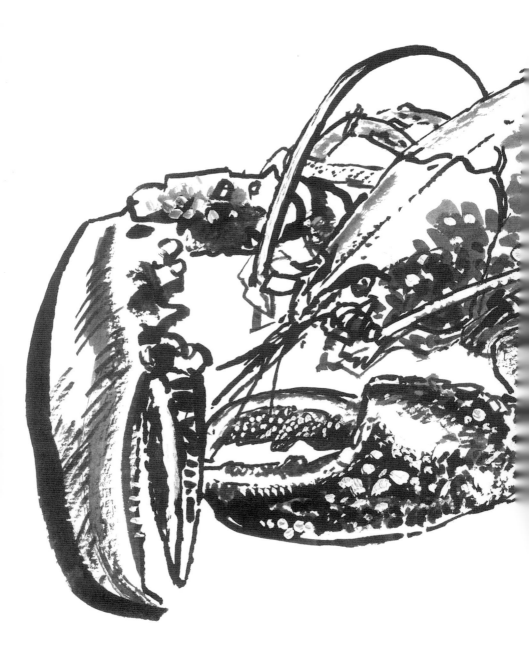

index

Sally & Stewart Walton have lived in Hastings for almost 25 years and written many books on craft, design and interiors. Fanatical about food, this is their third cookery book. Stewart is an illustrator and furniture designer working with recycled wood (recycledwood.org.uk) Sally designs and makes beautiful bags from rare vintage textiles (carry-a-bag.com).

Debi Angel settled in Hastings after years of weekending in Rye Harbour. Primarily known as a successful magazine design director, now freelance. She has a passion of typefaces and exhibits locally also as an artist. (debiangel.com)

SEA SAW BOOKS
www.seasawbooks.co.uk

SEA SAW BOOKS WOULD LIKE TO THANK:
LOUISE BELL for her hard work, editorial expertise and tact. Friends who contributed recipes and those who kindly checked the copy before it went to print. And of course, Hastings Printing Company Limited.